SON OF PERFECTION

Part One

By

Professor Hilton Hotema

978-1-63923-442-4

Printed: October 2022

Cover Art By: Amit Paul

Published and Distributed By:
Lushena Books
607 Country Club Drive, Unit E
Bensenville, IL 60106
www.lushenabks.com

ISBN: 978-1-63923-442-4

SON OF PERFECTION

By Prof. Hilton Hotema

(In Two Parts)

A Summary Of The Hidden Teachings Of The Apocalypse
(Last Book of the Bible)

Chapter	Title	

FOREWORD

Man is the subject of the Ancient Scriptures.

Perfect Man is the Hero of the Ancient Scriptures.

Deportment in harmony with Cosmic Law was the ancient standard of Perfect Man.

According to the principles of the Ancient Masters, complete self-mastery was their standard of Perfect Man. For he who conquers himself is greater than he who conquers a city.

He that overcometh the desires of the flesn and the passions of the blood, and obeyeth the commandment not to eat of the "forbidden fruit", the same shall inherit all things good in life; and I, Perfection, will be his Guide, and he shall be my Son (Gen. 2:17; Rev. 21:7).

The first book and the last book of the Bible deal with the "forbidden fruit". The last book describes, in symbol and parable, the nature of the man who heeds the commandment not to eat of the "forbidden fruit", and defines the great reward inherited by him for obedience. For such is the only man who is worthy to open the book and to loose the seals thereof (Rev. 5).

Also, in the last book of the Bible there is concealed the greatest of all secrets of the Human Body, the Microcosm. This secret, hidden in symbol and parable, is so strange and obscure that as yet modern science knowns nothing about it, and the priests and preachers have never discovered it.

The purpose of this work is to uncover and reveal that carefully guarded secret, in language so simple that it can be understood by an eight grade scholar.

CHAPTER NO. 1

Last--Strangest--Oldest

> Last book of the Bible
> Oldest book of the Bible
> Strangest book of the Bible

A book so strange that the best brains of the Christian world have never been able to interpert it.

A book so old that its origin is lost in the night of time.

A book so baffling that the church refused to let it become a part of the Bible until the 19th century; and then, for a most peculiar reason, it was embraced with open arms.

In the Bible this book is headed, "The Revelation of St. John the Divine." It purports to be a revelation by God to Jesus Christ; Jesus Christ to his "angel," and the "angel" to John, and John to the Seven Churches in Asia, -- and the churches rejected it as a fraud.

In referring to this book, Wm. McCarthy wrote: "The book is wholly a composition. Its material was taken from many sources, yet the compiler studiously refrains from indicating its source. In fact, he endeavors to make it appear the material was original with him" (Bible, Church and God, p. 691).

APOLLONIUS

The secret of this book and its source lie with that active man of the New Testament called Paul, whose real name was Apollonius, but his friends and followers called him Pol and Polos.

Apollonius was the greatest philosopher, mystic and magician of the first century, and he became the Mystery Man of the New Testament. When he visited India about 46 AD to study the Hindu religion and be initiated in the Indian Mysteries, he was given that Scroll which became the last book of the Bible.

What did he do with it? He brought it home with him, retired to the "isle that is called Patmos" (Rev. 1:9), and there he translated the scroll into his native tongue, revising it to make it harmonize with the conditions of his country and the customs of his people.

Conclusive evidence to prove that all references to the gospel Jesus in "The Revelation of St. John the Divine" are fraudulent interpolations, inserted by the church fathers to deceive the faithful masses, appears in the fact that the Hindu Masters produced the Scroll thousands of years before the world ever heard of that Jesus.

-2-

When Pol made his first copy of the Hindu Scroll he titled it "Initiation of Anointed Ieosus."

When the Greeks copied Pol's copy, they changed the title to "Apocalypse."

When the Greek copy was translated to English, the title was changed to "The Revelation," and "St. John The Divine" was presented as the author.

What was the original title of the Scroll?

When Pol copied the Scroll, his work shows he was not free of egotism. He studiously refrained from indicating its source, and carefully endeavored to make it appear the material was original with him, wrote McCarthy.

Pol inserted many changes in the context of the Scroll to disguise its true origin and make it appear as his own work. But he "let the cat out of the bag" when he had to go into the field of the Kundalini Power of the Hindus by including the BOOK WITH SEVEN SEALS (Rev. 5).

The Book with Seven Seals is definite, positive and conclusive evidence to prove the source of the Scroll. For most of the ancient Hindu scriptures revolve around the Seven Chakra of the Human Body.

It is conceded generally that the scriptures of the Brahmins are anterior to the oldest part of the Bible. The Vedas, Puranas, Upanishads, etc., are filled with fables relating to the body with its Seven Chakras, its organs, glands, and functions.

THE HINDU SCROLL

What happened to Pol's copy of the Hindu Scroll after his death about 98 AD? It was found by one Marcion at Ephesus, along with some of Pol's other writings, some of which were used by the clever Bible makers in compiling the New Testament. But they rejected this scroll, largely because its symbols and parables could not be comprehended.

REINCARNATION

The church authorities rejected the scroll as fraudulent. Luther doubted the scroll's inspiration. Erasmus and Swingli both rejected it. Calvin doubted it?

How was this opposition overcome, and the scroll, regarded as a fraud for sixteen hundred years, finally adopted by the church and included in the Bible?

A clever priest took charge of the rejected scroll. He studied it, and he saw in it things which would greatly redound to the benefit of the church, if properly presented. That was something always welcomed by the church.

The Ancient Masters taught the Doctrine of Reincarnation. In fact, it was such common knowledge in those days that it was always treated as exoteric in all archaic religions and philosophies. Knowledge of its truth, on a basis of personal experience, was one of the first results obtained by him who entered upon the initial stages of the telestic work.

Whether the doctrine is true or false is beside the point here, as we are following the ancient teachings.

Reincarnation played a leading role in this Hindu scroll. It was that return of Solar Man to a future incarnation which made the clever priest see what he saw.

He saw that he could produce a translation of the scroll, have it appear as "The Revelation of Jesus Christ, which God gave unto him" (Rev. 1:1) and then by a little more twisting and distorting, make the return of Solar Man to a future incarnation appear as THE SECOND COMING OF CHRIST.

The first millennium had come and gone and the Christ so diligently expected had failed to appear. So now the time was ripe to prepare the mind of the gullible masses for the "Second Coming" at the end of the next millennium. Why not? That would hold them in line a little longer.

So the cunning priest made his translation say: "For the time is at hand." "Behold, he (Christ) cometh with clouds; and every eye shall see him, and they also which pierced him: and all kindreds of the earth shall wail because of him" (Rev. 1:3, 7).

Then he went all out in the 20th chapter and made it amazing by itself:

"And I saw thrones, and they sat upon them, and judgment was given unto them: and I saw the souls of them that were beheaded for the witness of Jesus, and, for the word of God, and which had not worshipped the beast, neither his image, neither had received his mark upon their foreheads, or in their hands; and they lived and reigned with Christ a thousand years" (Rev. 20:4).

When this revised and perfected translation was placed before the church authorities in the 19th century, it was quickly accepted with open arms; and that is how -- --

The strangest book of the Bible:
The Oldest book of the Bible,
     Came to be
The last book of the Bible.

And this Hindu scroll, less than two centuries ago, was made the last book of the Bible; for it had to come after the New Testament so the gospel Jesus could be made the Hero of it.

Then with the ancient writings destroyed, the church never suspected that

-4-

any one, clergyman or layman, would ever be able to interpret the strange symbols and allegories of the scroll.

MARCION

The man Mark of the second gospel of the Bible is termed by history the Father of Christianity. It would be more correct to term him the Father of the New Testament, translated by him from the writings of Apollonius.

This man was one Marcion, a native of Cappadocia, a small country in Asia Minor, adjoined on the side by the smaller country of Calicia, which borders on the Mediterranean Sea and touches the Gulf of Issus, on which gulf is the city of Tarsus, home of Saul, later called Paul, who said:

"I am a Jew of Tarsus, a city of Cilicia, ...yet brought up in this city (Jerusalem) at the feet of Gameliel, and taught according to the perfect manner of the law of the fathers" (Acts 7:58; 21:39; 22:3).

Marcion was an educated and influential Cappadocian, and spoke the Samaritan language, the same as Apollonius.

Like all men, he was looking for fame and fortune. He had heard of the great work of Apollonius, and about thirty years after the latter's death, he went to Ephesus and Antioch and collected what he could find of the writings of Apollonius, among which was the Hindu scroll.

These writings were in the Smaritan tongue, and were not available to the Greek and Latin scholars of the time.

Pol (Apollonius) was the Father of Christianity, as it was he who produced the writings that become the New Testament. But it was Marcion who translated them into Greek, and began the work that laid the foundation of the N.T. That is the reason why he is called the Father of Christianity.

As Marcion worked on these writings, he discovered that they contained secrets of Life not known by the world at large. He saw that this fact presented a rare opportunity to make him great, and he grabbed it. That was about 130 AD.

Charles B. Waite, a fearless and tireless searcher for truth, showed beyond all question in his "History of Christianity to 200 AD" that the gospel of Marcion was the original work from which the four N. T. gospels were later fabricated by the biblical plagiarists. He demonstrated that the author of the Mark and Luke gospels and the Pauline Epistles were one and the same person.

According to Marcion, the real foundation of the Pauline Epistles, as he copied and translated them, "was the sign of the Zodiac known as Aries, the Ram or Lamb. The early Christians all worshipped a lamb instead of a man on a cross" (Ant. Unv. p. 154).

This statement is supported by the further fact that at the Sixth Ecumenical Council held at Constantinople in the year 680 AD, it was ordained end decreed "that in place of a lamb, the figure of a man should be portrayed on the Cross" (Ant. Unv. p. 161).

When Marcion translated the Hindu scroll into Greek, he found its symbols and allegories too deep for him to fathom, so he lay it aside as usless to him.

But it was fortunate for the seekers of truth that the Greek translation of the scroll preserved its true and correct contents, and shows how greatly the clever priest distorted the scroll in order to make it acceptable to the church authorities as part of the Bible.

APOCALYPSE

In the old Greek translation the title of the scroll was simply "Apocalypse, a Greek word meaning to reveal, to disclose, to disrobe, to unveil, and that was the reason why the clever priest translated the title "Revelation," — yet to the clergy it reveals no more than it did to Marcion; and Isis wrapped in her peplum was never more safe from the eyes of the world than is the inner meaning of the Apocalypse.

Fundamentally, the Apocalypse is a fable. It is one of the most stupendous fables ever written. So comprehensive, complete and coherent is the fable, that its full beauty, even its fine finish of details, can be perceived only when viewed in its entirety.

Nor can its esoteric meaning be grasped by mere analytical study. Its multiplicity of details and reduplication of symbols have utterly exotericists have fared even worse thru their inability to distinguish from the main acion of the fable the explanatory matter introduced as side-scenes.

The Hero of the fable is Solar Man; and the context of the fable describes the conquest of Physical Man by Solaricel Man.

The description of tha struggle is fabulized in terms of cosmic phenomena because it relates to cosmic production and treats of cosmic processes. The substance of the description lies beyond the understanding of all who are not well-versed in the secrets of occultism and the details of metaphysics

The details of the fable present, in symbol and parable, the sensations and emotions which are experienced by Solar Man as ha tremblingly goes thru the various ordeals of the solemn ceremony of Initiation in the Higher life, as taught in the Sacred Ancient Mysteries, and as we explained in our work titled the "MYSTERIOUS SPHINX" (pp. 27-30).

It is similar to an attempt to describe the sensations and emotions of a candidate who goes thru the various ordeals of the ceremony of Initiation in the Masonic Lodge and do it in symbol and parable.

What relation would that have to Christianity? to religion? to theology? or to heaven? Yet that is exactly what and all the Apocalypse is --a description by the Ancient Masters in symbol and parable, of the strange sensations and emotions experienced by the neophyte as his mind and body react and respond to the strange things he encounters in the various tests to which he is subjected in the ordeals of initiation in the Ancient Mysteries.

That is the reason why Pol titled his copy of the scroll "Initiation of Anointed Ieosus." For that is the correct title.

And furthermore, these psychic emotions and physical sensations are skillfully presented in terms of cosmic phenomena,--as the flashing glare of lightning, the crashing roll of thunder, the quivering shock of the earthquake, and the ceaseless murmur of the waters.

THE ANCIENT WISDOM

We move into the very midst of the Mystery of Man as we approach the border line of the Living World, so cleverly portrayed in symbol and parable in the Hindu Scroll.

As the great Carrel clearly showed the world in his remarkable book, "Man The Unknown" that modern doctors do not possess the psychobio-physiological knowledge of man that is necessary for a survey of the Apocalypse, we are certain that the layman does .not.

Therefore, a brief sketch, in simple terms, will be given of the topics that must be considered and reviewed in the interpretation of this Hindu Scroll.

First, the point where the ancient arcane system sharply diverges from all conventional schools of thought, is in the means of acquiring knowledge.

Conventional scientist and orthodox religionists rely for knowledge on the physical senses, psychic emotions, and intellectual faculties as they are in the present state of human development and human degeneration.

The scientist enlarges the scope of the senses by the use of microscope, telescope, and other mechanical devises, but these can never reach beyond the material.

The religionist puts his faith in ancient scriptures which have been distorted by the church, and which are misleading to the exoteric because they were not written to be understood by any one but the initiates. That is the reason why this Hindu Scroll cannot be interpreted by the clergy.

The esotericist refuses to be confined within the narrow limits of the five senses and the mental faculties. He realized that the gnostic powers of Solar Man are hopelessly obstructed by the imperfect instrument, the physical organism, the material garment in which he is clad and thru which he must function; so he devotes himself to whay may be termed intensive self-evolution, the conquest and utilization of all the forces and faculties that lie latent in that fontal essence within his own body, which is the primary source of all the elements and powers of his Being, of all that he is, has been, and will be. THAT MYSTERIOUS KINGDOM WITHIN.

By raising his state of consciousness, and by gaining conscious control of the concealed potencies that are the proximate cause of his individual evolution, the esotericist seeks to tread the path that leads to solar illumination and spiritual liberation from physical bondage, moving forward, as it were, toward that goal which mankind, as a whole, will never reach, because great skill, knowledge and perseverance are required to aid the Seeker of Light in avoiding the snares and traps placed along the path by tyrants and their hencemen.

The difficult task of the Seeker of Light is not so much to know as to become. To know is easier than to become. Many know, but lack the will-power to become.

Herein lies the powerful import of the Delphic inscription, "Know Thy Self," and the ancient admonition, He that overcometh the desires and passions of the flesh, and obeyeth the command not to eat of the "forbidden fruit," the same shall inherit all things good in life; and I (Perfection) will be his Guide, and he shall be my son (Gen. 2:17; Rev. 21:7).

Regardless of the profundity of our knowledge, if not intelligently and persistently applied, it is worthless.

The esotericist understands that true self-knowledge can be attained by only through self-development and self-conquest in the highest sense of the terms,--a development that begins with the conquest of pernicious habits and leads on to a healthy body and an introspection and the awakening of the regenerative forces which slumber in civilized man's inner protoplasmic nature, like the vivific potency in the female ovum, which, when activated, transforms man into a divine being.

This course of transecendental self-conquest, the development of man from the concealed essence of his own embryonic nature of a self-luminous, immortal being, is the sole subject matter of the Hindu scroll, which contains, in symbol and parable, an almost complete outline of the psycho-bio-physiological process of Redemption.

If the misled clergy knew aught of man's psycho-bio-physiological constitution, they would never attempt to interpret the Apocalypse as treating of "heaven and the church."

THE MICROCOSM

Everything contained in the Universe is contained in man. In our work titled COSMIC CREATION we wrote, "Man's body is a mass of billions of cells, each of which is a mass of millions of atoms, each of which is a globular system with planets whirling with tremendous speed" (p. 4).

Analogous to the Universe or Macrocosm, the Microcosm (man) has four departments which correspond with the Four Cosmic Principles of which the world consists,--Fire, Air, Water, and Earth, as told by us in "THE MYST-ERIOUS SPHINX" (p. 27).

These four Principles appear in man as follows: Earth constitutes the physical body, which is interpenetrated by the fluidal body, and these two are interpenetrated by the aerial body, and these are engenered and sustained by the solar (fire) body, as we have stated in "THE MYSTERIOUS SPHINS" (p. 34).

The fourth body (solar electricity) constitutes what we term the Life Principle, and is called Solar Man, the Real Man, the Ego, the Nous.

SOLAR MAN

Solar Man is the living, conscious, vital electricity, of incredible voltage but not comparable to the form of electricity known to physicists. A definite phase of this force is what the Hindus term the Kundalini Fire. It is polarized, the positive phase being termed the "good serpent" in ancient symbology, and the negative phase being termed the "bad serpent", as explained by us in THE MAGIC WAND.

In the telestic work, or cycle of initiation, this force weaves from the primal substance of the auric ovum, according to the ideal form or archetype it contains, and conforming thereto, the Immortal Augoeides, or Solar Body (Soma Heliakon), so-called because in its visible appearance it is self-luminous like the sun. with a golden radiance. Its aureola displays an opalescence.

This Solar Body (Man) is of atomic, non-molecular substance, and impossible to describe because our language is formed to describe the physical and not the solarical.

The psychic (lunar) body, through which Solar Man functions in the psychic realm, is molecular in structure, but of much finer substance than the elements composing the gross physical body, to which organism is closely responds, having organs that match the physical senses, which, in fact, are the exteriorized representatives of the psychic body.

In appearance, the psychic body has a silvery luster, tinged with delicate violet; and its aura is of palest blue, with an interchanging play of all the prismatic colors, rendering it irridescent.

In our interpretation of the Hindu scroll, we must observe a certain fourth body mentioned in mystic writings. In Sanskrit it is called Kama Rupa, the form engendered by lust. It comes into existence only after somatic death, save in the exceptional cases of the extremely evil socerer, who has become morally dead while physically alive.

The Ancient Masters said that this body is of phantasm shape, from the dregs and effluvia of matter by the image-creating power of the gross animal mind, which rules the desire to procreate on the animal plane. and which is purely an animal function and can never be anything more.

Of such nature are the "unclean spirits" of the New Testament, where also the "abominable stench" seems to be a convert allusion to this malodorous shade.

This phantasm has the shadowy semblance of the physical body from which it was derived, and is surrounded by a cloudy sure of brick-red hue.

CYCLES OF LIFE

In the esoteric cosmogony the theory of "dead" matter has no place.

The Universe is a manifestation of life, or consciousness, from the Sun down to the very atoms of the material elements, as we have explained in "THE KINGDOM OF HEAVEN" (p. 12).

In the Ancient Wisdom a sharp distinction was made between Being and Existence.

The Archetypal World is that of True Being, changeless, external; while existence is a moving outward into the worlds of becoming, of ceaseless change and transformation.

The Universe and all its parts move in cycles, according to law. Solar Man is ruled by this law, and in his case it is termed the Law of Reincarnation.

According to the Masters, Solar Man enters upon a cycle of incarnations, passing in due order from one mortal body to another, leaving the old and building a new one.

The material body, according to the Masters, is a temporary dwelling place on the earth plane of Solar Man (1 Cor. 3:16), which has fashioned that form, leaves it in due course, and builds another, repeating that process over and over for seven times, in harmony with the cosmic Law of Seven. But the time between incarnations may cover a period extending from a century to a millennium.

This ancient doctrine of reincarnation had always prevailed throughout the world, except in modern times, when it was cast into darkness by the Roman State Church in order to believe in its "Lord and Savior Jesus Christ."

It was taught by Phthagoras and Plato; it was one of the principles of the Druid faith. Caesar found it among the Gauls. It was found in the old races of Mexico, Central and South America.

Among modern philosophers, Kant and Scopenhauer upheld it. Bruno, Goethe and Emerson found it agreeable to their thoughts. Mystics and poets have professed faith in it. Huxley, the archpriest of mid-Victorian materalistic science, wrote of it:

"None but very hasty thinkers will reject it on the ground of inherent absurdity. The doctrine has its roots in the world of reality, and it can claim such support as the great argument of analogy is capable of supplying."

Eternal life, interrupted physically by somatic death and resumed from one physical existence to another, would explain better than any other theory, the vast difference between persons of the same families, in the kind and degree of their abilities, capacities, and the conditions of their existehce.

On what other interpretation of cosmic processes than that presented by reincarnation, is it possible to discover any semblance of essential justice; or account for the feeling that we all have had at one time or another, of "I have been here before," or "This has been thus before," as expressed by Rosetti in "Sudden Light".

In no other theory are explicable the secret likings and Antipathies that urge men to seek out their fate; the haunting charm to the eye of certain faces; to the ear of certain voices; the kinship to the mind of certain fields of knowledge--different fields to different minds--or the vividness of the imagination of particular periods of past history.

It is an axiom of science that, in the absence of evidence which is conclusive, that theory is best which most completely and successfully accounts for and correlates the greatest number of unexplained phenomena.

The ancient teaching to the effect that man, thru successive incarnations, is self-rewarded, self-punished, reaps as he sows, and builds, good or bad, the material body he inhabits; that failure is at most only postponement, and success but a stepping-stone to greater effort, satisfies not only the head but the heart also.

When Krishnamurti was asked about reincarnation, he said, "Reincarnation is a fact, and what good will that do you now?"

No doubt he meant to imply that preoccupation with one's past or future diverts the mind from concentration on the NOW, which is the only point of contact with physical reality and the only door thru which any newness may enter,

It is fairly well established that past and future are illusions of the objective consciousness, which creates its otwn time element. Of this Ouspensky wrote:

We know already by our intellect that everything exists in infinite spaces of time--nothing is made, nothing becomes, all is" (Tertium Organum).

The Universe is a unit. It had no beginning and has no end. All things in it partake of that same perpetual quality.

Solar Man is an eternal as the stars. His own ignorance makes his own limitations which rise from mind control, faulty education, and all other measures designed by tyrants to fit man in the social pattern which constitutes modern civilizztion, the preservation of which order requires that all knowledge must be curtailed and controlled.

As physical existence is Time for man, as he is embedded in it, and as false teaching keeps him in darkness as to himself, he cannot realize by experience the truth of that which his intellect assures him, nor conceive of himself otherwise than as conditioned by Time. In truth, for him, Time is not. For him, Time does not exist any more than it does for the Sun.

CHAPTER NO. 2

SEVEN INCARNATIONS

The Apocalypse is based on the doctrine that at least Seven Incarnations are required for the attainment of that higher state of consciousness which was the goal of the Masters.

Physics provides an excellent analogy for this understanding: When heat is applied to solid substance, while its temperature rises, to all external appearance it remains the same,

But the moment the degree of heat is reached which marks the melting point of that particular substance, it begins to change to liquid, which changes its shape and seemingly its very nature.

That same kind of transformation occurs when visible liquid changes into invisible gas, and the once solid substance is now floating in the invisible world,--but it still is.

These natural changes are produced by expansion of the molecules and an increase in the vibratory rate of the constituent particles of any given substance, whether it be the trunk of a tree or a human body. Nothing comes to an end. Everything that is, is eternal.

Yoga is like that. It is a self-induced raising of one's rate of vibration, with the result that when the rate reaches a certain intensity, there ensues an expansion of Consciousness which effects a change of state, a release of power, a freedom of movement in a more ample medium, in which the element of Time disappears, or changes to something else, and physical laws, known to us, fade into spiritual laws unknown to physical man.

While the heating process for man may be a slow one, resumed and repeated life after life (as no necessary steps can be omitted), the final apotheosis may be sudden and surprising, like the sudden volatilization of liquid into gas.

This phase of the subject is mentioned in the Apocalypse as follows: "Behold, I cam quickly....Behold I come quickly; and my reward is with me.. He which testifieth these things saith, Surely I come quickly" (Rev. 3:11; 22:7, 12, 20).

Then the clever priest added this spurious interpolation, "Even so, come Lord Jesus" (Rev. 22:20).

The Ancient Masters taught that the telestic work had for its object the achievement of deliverance from the ordeal of Renicarnation, holding that this is complete and final only when the external Solar Body is completely individualized, which is the production of Perfect Man who is thereby freed from further processes of reincarnation in the mortal physical and psychic forms.

This is a very difficult subject to put into simple language, and in spite of our simplification of it, not many are competent to comprehend it, which is another example to show how far advanced were the Ancient Masters.

THE MATERIAL GARMENT

In elucidating the Hindu scroll, the Material Garment worn by Solar Man in the visible world must be noticed somewhat in detail.

The Material Temple in which Solar Man dwells may be considered an objective microcosm, an epitome of the Universe, to evey department of which the organs and functions of the Material Temple correspond and are in direct relation.

Furthermore, as the material object thru which Solar Man contacts the visible world, its organs correspond to, and are the respective instruments of, the powers and faculties of Solar Man.

Thus the physical body has four chief vital centers that are analogues of the Four Cosmic Principles described in our work "The Mysterious Sphins," and of the four manifested generic powers of Solar Man. These four somatic divisions are:

1. Brain, seat of the higher mind.
2. Lungs and heart, seat of the lower mind.
3. Navel region, center of the passional nature.
4. Generative center, seat of the vivifying powers on the animal plane.

For the purpose at hand, it is unnecessary to go deeper into details as to these correspondences, save only as to the nerve system and the solar force operating thru it.

The nerve system is a unit with dual aspects as follows:

1. The cerebro-spinal, consisting of brain and spinal cord.
2. The sympathetic or ganglionic department.

While virtually distinct, these two systems are intimately related in their ramifications of the body and are powdered by the same force.

The sympathetic system consists of a series of distinct nerve-centers, or ganglia, consisting of small masses of vascular neurine, extending on each side of the spinal column from the head to the coccyx or base of the spine.

ASTRAL PLANE

As long as modern science refuses to recognize planes of existence beyond the material, and as long as theology remains in its darkness, the masses will never realize the greatness of the Ancient Masters.

No understanding of the recondite phases of the Hindu scroll is possible for those with little knowledge of the structures and functions of the body, and especially those organs that function in correspondence with planes of existence beyond the material.

For be it known that the body's organs and glands must and do function in correspondence with every plane of existence. That is the ancient secret that stops modern critics cold in their tracks when they attempt to interpret the symbols and parables of the Hindu scroll.

In addition to the glands that function in harmony with the material plane, the Masters taught that man has an occult, astral or fourth dimensional body that functions in correspondence with the fourth dimensional plane, about which modern science knows nothing, and which we have discussed in our work title KINGDOM OF HEAVEN (p. 35).

It was that secret to which the Ancient Masters referred when they said that the Kingdom of Heaven is within (Lu. 17:21).

Ancient allegories contain many references to the Astral Plane, which modern acientists refuse to recognize, and concerning which modern theology has no clear conception. So, we must consider this phase of the subject in order to understand the baffling parables of the Hindu scroll.

According to the Masters, there are Seven Planes of Existence. The lowest is the material, the next is that known as the Plane of Force; the third as the Astral, and the fourth as the Mental Plane.

In addition to these four, there are three higher ones known to advanced occultists. They have no names that can be understood by the masses, and the terms are incapable to explanation to those who live on the lower planes.

In fact, there are but few of the controlled minds that are competent to break the bonds of the social pattern and grasp many of the things which we have described as simply as possible in this work.

We must first form a clear conception of the term "plane". If one consults

-14-

dictionaries one usually gets the impression that planes are places or series of level layers, or strata.

That is wrong, and that error rises from the mistake of considering planes as composed of matter, It is all a matter of vibration. The densest form of matter, stone and steel, is just a mass of vibratory waves.

Material man is a mass of vibratory waves. So is Solar Man.

Dr. H. H. Sheldon, University of New York, said:

"Electrons, long thought to be the ultimate particles of which all matter is formed, have now been shown to have a reality only as a wave form, while an atom consists of a bundle of such waves.

"We as individuals undoubtedly have no existence in reality, other than as waves,--multitudinous and complicated centers, perhaps, in what is called the ether" (We Do Not Die, p. 13).

Planes do nor rise one above the other. They are graded as to their respective degrees of vibration. They are Planes of Vibration, and not Planes of Matter. Matter is the lowest degree of vibration.

The various planes have not spatial distinction nor degree. They interpenetrate one another in the same point of space. A single point of space may have its manifestations of all the seven planes of being.

Mack Stauffer, "The World's Greatest Second-Sightest," wrote: "Man is a creature of vibratory-impressions only. In the material world he is a creature of but five sense-impressions. namely: Seeing, hearing, tasting, smelling and touching,--but there are perhaps 500 other senses used by the insects" (Mass-Intellectual Pressure, p. 12).

The main reason why the Hindu scroll was so darkly veiled is because it treats of the mysteries of the Seven Senses of Man, mentioned often in allegorical form in the Bible.

ASTRAL BODY

Man corresponds to all planes of existence. His astral body corresponds to the astral plane.

The sense powers of the physical body have their astral counterparts, and function on the astral plane as the physical function on the physical plane.

The Masters knew and taught that man has seven senses instead of five.

Solomon's temple had an approach consisting of 5 and 7 steps. Jesus fed the multitude on 5 loaves and 2 fishes at one time, and the fragments left filled 12 baskets (Mat. 14:17-20). At another time he gave the multitude 7 loaves and a few little fishes, and the fragments remaining filled 7 baskets (Mat. 15:34-37).

These fives represent the sense powers of the average man of darkness, and the sevens represent the seven sense powers of the Seer. The twelves represent the 12 signs of the Zodiac.

Heed not the dead letter of the Bible. Look for the hidden meaning. The dead letter does not make sense, but the hidden meaning in the message reveals a deep secret of Life.

The two higher sense powers are dormant or semi-dormant in the average person, and need to be "resurrected from the dead". They have their astral counterparts

Those who have been blessed with extra good health and developed the powers of astral vision, are able to perceive the scenes of the astral plane as clearly as those of the material, and as the Indians of South America, mentioned in our work "KINGDOM OF HEAVEN" (p. 19-21).

The great Apollonius, while preaching in Ephesus, saw in Rome the assassination of the Emperor Domitian, described in our work "MYSTERY MAN OF THE BIBLE".

The common claivoyant has flashes of astral vision, but is not able to sense astrally by act of will. The trained occultist is able to shift from one set of sense powers to the other as he desires. He may function on both planes at the same time, as in the case of Apollonius.

The Hindu Masters taught that the Astral Body of man contains 420,000 nadis, or nerves, two of which are termed major, and a more important third one (Sushumna), that runs relative to the spinal column, extending from the Pons Varoli of the brain to the Muladhare chakra ("root support") at the base of the spine.

The other two nadis terminate in the Prostate Gland (Svadhishtan chakra) slightly above the Maladhara. The symbolic figure in the pericarp is a crescent, representing water, Aquarius, waterman, human head of the Sphinx, which corresponds to Sagittarius of the Zodiac; hence its regent is the Bowman.

The Yogins called this gland the Kanda, the seat of the Kudalini Power, termed by them the Mother of the Universe, and about which Rishi Singh Gherwal wrote:

"The Kundalini, Divine Mother, always keeps for herself a chosen country, in which her Higher Wisdom is preserved from all danger. That land is India" (Kundalini, p. 11), and India is the home of the Hindu scroll.

The two major nadis mentioned are the Ida (moon tube, cooling) and Pingala (sun tube, heating).

The Ida extends from the Kanda to the left nostril, after crossing over from the right side; and the Pingala extends from the Kanda to the right nostril, after crossing over from the left side.

We are told that these two nadis must be emptied of their Pranic force, which thence passes to the Sushumna, before the Kundalini can be made to rise. Then the Kundalini passes up thru the Sushumna, the Kulamarga, Royal Road, or Brahmanadi. Tube of Brahma.

It is said that as the Prana of the air passes into the nose, it causes a tiny valve at the root of the nostrils to open, and as the air gases pass into the lungs, a certain force in the air called Prana. passes down the Ida and Pingala nadis to the Kanda.

A STARTLING DISCOVERY

The Western World little knows that concealed in that Hindu Scroll is the greatest of all secrets of the Human Body.

This secret, described in symbol and parable in "The Revelation", is so deep and so mysterious, that as yet modern science knows nothing about it.

The Book with Seven Seals is the evidence to prove that the Scroll originally came from India. That book represents the Human Body, and the Seven Seals represent the Seven Cells of that Cosmic Battery contained in the body.

Medical art, with all its boasting, knows so little about this Vital Battery, that when some of its parts were first discovered a few years ago, the "wise" doctors just snipped them out and threw them away, as useless and worthless. The sad victims of this stupid work lived just as long as it took them to die.

A chart of the Vital Battery and its Seven Cells is concealed in the Apocalypse.

The battery is charged with Cosmic Radiation, Solar Electricity, Vital Force —— called Prana by the Hindus.

The great secret of this Battery is the fact that when its force is not dissipated, when that force is conserved, increased and intensified by certain secret methods discovered by the Hindu Masters, then man's state of Consciousness is vastly augmented, to the point where ——

THERE IS NOTHING COVERED, THAT SHALL NOT BE REVEALED; AND NOTHING HID, THAT SHALL NOT BE KNOWN (Mat. 10:26).

The remarkable success of Chiropractic is due to the fact that the manipulations of the spinal column by the Chiropractor stimulate the cells of the battery and increase the flow of cosmic electricity (nerve force) to the various organs and glands.

All traces of this the greatest secret of the body might have been lost to the Western World, had that precious Hindu Scroll not been brought to Asia Minor by Poll, and included in the Christian Bible. And to this day the church and the clergy are unaware of the secret concealed in the Apocalypse.

Solar Chambers

In part II of our "COSMIC SCIENCE" we have discussed at length the body's glands and solar chambers, and by reading that the student will acquire a better knowledge of his conscious powers.

He will there learn that the solar chambers in his ears are ruined by poluted air while he is still a child; that eating salt ruins his Thymus and other delicate and important glands; and that ---

His function of breathing is analogous to the Great Fiery Breath of Universe, which builds Nature in the exhalation process, and at the end of each Grand Cycle, involving eons of time, the process reverses and sucks back into the Cosmic Reservoir all visible things called Nature, and these recede and disappear in regular order in the Grand Cosmic Cycle, and return to Absolutism, the primal source whence they come, and there to remain for renovation and purification, and then to flow forth again at the dawn of the next Cosmic Day.

Two of the most important glands, or cells, of the Vital Battery, are located in the skull, and, in connection with them, there are Five Solar Chambers in the skull which must function harmoniously and synchronously with the cells in order to raise man to the superior state of Cosmic Consciousness.

These chambers, the functions of which is unknown to modern science, were by the Maters called the Five Stars of the Microcosm, and are symbolized in ancient scriptures as the Five Golden Emerods (1 S. 6:4), the Five Loaves, (Mat. 14:17), etc.

The Sankhys doctrine states that the Five Senses are the exterior products of the five corresponding Solarical centers, which are named as follows:

1. Frontal Sinus, a cavity in the frontal bone of the skull.
2. Sphenoidal Sinus, a cavity in the sphenoid bone of the skull.
3. Maxillary Sinus, largest of the five, and resembles a pyramid.
4. Palatine Sinus, a cavity in the orbital process of the palatine bone and opening into either the sphenoidal or a posterior ethmoidal sinus.
5. Ethnoidal Sinus, this chamber consists of numerous small cavities occupying the labyrinth of the ethmod bone, and in these cavities are situated the small, mysterious glands known in Occult Science as the Intellectual Organs.

The Sinuses communicate directly or indirectly with the nasal cavity; and it is significant to observe that they receive the Breath of Life directly and unmodified as it flows in from the universe to then thru the nose, and before any of the other air organs have a chance to select and absorb any substance from the Solar Essence of the Cosmos, charged with every known and unknown element.

-18-

The Sinuses are lined with mucous membrane extending into them from the nose, and to them rapidly spreads all disorders that effect the nose. They receive without protection the full force of all poisonous gases and acids in the air.

The nose is the first organ damaged by polluted air, and the first reaction is called a "cold" which medical art considers a very simple ailment.

The world would be shocked if it know the whole truth. That cold is tne first symptom which shows that the glands of the higher conscious powers are suffering damage from which they will never fully recover.

The inflammation of the nasal mucous lining extends into the Sinuses, and then appear the pains, -headache (frontal sinus), and deep seated pains back of eyes (sphenoidal sinus).

These aches and pains, considered so lightly by medical art, indicate serious damage being done to these Electric Chambers, caused by polluted air.

Thus begins the destruction of the higher conscious powers of man, while he is still an infant, a child. When the facts are known, that "cold" is not so simple as medical art thinks.

The mucus excretions of the lining of the maxillary sinus in inflammatory conditions, fill up the cavity of this sinus, as the orifice is at the upper most part. Such of the mucus as cannot be blown out thru the nose, remains in the sinus, where it gradually hardens, destroying the electrical function of that chamber on the higher plane, ---the largest of the group.

No Full Recovery from Ailments

Full recovery from disorders is another medical myth. Each one is a step down the ladder of degeneration to the grave at the bottom. If the illness is slight, the damage is slight; if severe, the damage done is severe.

Recovery from each illness is only partial, regardless of how slight the illness may be. But if degeneration goes not too far, a change in environment and in one's mode of living that brings the body into harmony with the cosmic law of life, will result in regeneration.

The sinuses superficially appear to medical art as nothing more then air chambers in the skull.

We remember that when medical art first found some of the parts of the Vital Battery, they were considered useless and worthless, and were cut out and thrown away.

Medical art treats as heathenish superstition the higher conscious powers of the body described in symbol and parable in ancient scriptures, It knows nothing of the higher function of the sinuses, and assumes that their purpose is to lend resonance to the voice.

Atomic Intelligence

Occult Science, termed by science as "that school of stupid superstition," teaches that in these Electrical Chambers is located the seat of the Atomic Intelligence of Man, mentioned by us in "KINGDOM OF HEAVEN" (p. 11). These air chambers, and the small glands in them, constitute the solarical sense-centers that receive Atomic Intelligence which is too subtle for contact by the five sense organs of man in his present degenerate state.

Into these chambers there incessantly flows a peculiar essence, termed by the Masters "Mental Spirit," but which is actually the cosmic intelligence of the Atom. It can produce no normal reaction in the electric chambers of civilized man, as they are damaged and crippled by polluted air.

The small glands, the Intellectual Organs, located in the skull near the point where the nose joins the forehead, are stimulated by the Atomic Force that passes thru the nostrils. Some term this force "free electrons."

In wild birds and beasts, and wild men that have not been tinged and tainted by the "blessings" of civilization, these solar centers are functionally developed,--and modern science attempts to explain the "uncanny" brain powers of these creatures by asserting that they are the result of "instinct"; but we are not told what "instinct" is.

If hunting dogs are kept in the house and breathe the stagnant, polluted air as the members of the family do, in time the nerves in the nose and sinuses become dull, and the dogs lose their keen sense of smell and are unable to trail game. Like causes produce like effects.

In our work titled "THE KINGDOM OF HEAVEN" we mentioned the wild Indians of South America who still possess the peculiar brain powers of early man, and of wild birds and beasts.

The polluted air of our wonderful civilization has not yet reached them, and their higher centers of Cosmic Intelligence are not dormantized and rendered practically useless by the destructive action of polluted air, in which civilized man ignorantly lives and sweatingly labors from birth to death.

If we were deaf and could not hear, and also blind and could not see, we would still be alive, but our world would be much smaller, and these conscious powers would be unknown to us. We would be an entity of only three senses.

Just as the melodies of music and the colors of cloth would be unknown to the blind and deaf, so are the mysteries of the higher world unknown to the man of only five sneses.

Our solar chambers are damaged by polluted air which we are still a little child and the chambers are embryonic, rudimentary, undeveloped,--and that is the end of our higher powers of consciousness.

That condition is so regular and so common in civilization, that exceedingly few ever escape the disaster. Those who do, exhibit the high powers of clairaudience, clairvoyance, and premonition. They are so few in number and so strange in deportment that they are suspiciously regarded as "freaks," and dangerous to the community.

Some of this class used to be condemned and put to death as "witches,"-- illustrating the grave danger one invites when so imprudent and indiscreet as to exhibit overtly the higher powers of consciousness.

The open study of psychology, especially in its wider sense and above the five-sense-power-level, was impossible in the dark ages. Torture and the stake awaited the investigators. Even today, considered an age of nelightenment, the open study of psychology is under suspicion.

If one appears now with the higher powers of consciousness, one must be silent for the sake of safety.

Long ages of degeneration have produced a very low standard of Life, but regardless of its lowness, if one rises above it one is in danger. If the physician rises above the standard of his profession, his license is promptly revoked for "unethical conduct." To be safe, one must conform to the low, rigid. orthodox pattern.

Under "Active Kundalini" we shall discuss the peculiar blending of the functions of seeing and hearing into a single sense as the result of the activation of certain brain centers, so that man is able to interpret, in his mind, the atomic vibrations of sight the same as he does those of sound, and vice versa.

It is all a matter of vibration, with our various sense organs reacting differently according to their constitution.

This is the true explanation of the "uncanny" sense powers of certain Indians of South America, and also of that great Master, Apollonius, who "saw" the assassination of Domitian in Rome while preaching at Ephesus, many miles away (Mystern Man of The Bible, - p. 18).

As the electric chambers in his skull, his cosmic radio and television mechanism, had not been damaged and ruined by the poisonous acids and gases in the air of civilization, so shockingly and convincingly described by Dr. Klamonti in his great work, "Man's Unused Powers," Apollonius was competent to interpret, in his mind, the atomic vibrations that these chambers received of the unusual disturbance in Rome.

Book With Seven Seals

We come now to that strange Book With Seven Seals mentioned in the Hindu Bcroll, which "no man in heaven, nor in earth. neither under the earth, was able to open, neither to look thereon" (Rev. 5:5).

What a mystery. A very strange "book" indeed. Some enigma for the masses, and some puzzle for the preachers.

The Book is the human body, and the Seven Seals are the Seven Cells of the Vital Battery, called chakras, being seven special nerve plexuses, thru which the Sushumna passes, and by the Hindus listed as follows:

1 Muladhara (sacral plexus)
2. Svadbishthana (prostatic plexus)
3. Manipuraka (solar plexus)
4. Anahate (cardiac plexus)
5. Vishuddhi (pharyngeal plexus)
6. Ajna (cavernous plexus)
7. Sahasrara (coranium plexus)

As the symbols and parables of Revelation deal with these Seven Cells of the Human Battery, the student should familiarize himself with them. For here we have the top secret of all the teachings of the Masters so cleverly concealed in the Bible, and seriously distorted by the makers of the Bible.

1. The Muladhara is the sacrel plexus, the lowest cell of the battery, lying at the root of the spinal column (Meru). This chakra is pictured as a lotus with four petals. In the pericarp is the figure of a square or cube that represents the Earth Element. The color of this lotus is yellow, for such is said to be the earth color.

2. The svadhishthana is the prostatic plexus, situated in the pelvic region, on a level with the root of the male organ of generation. It is the   six -petalled lotus. In the pericarp is a crescent, representing water. The color of this chakra is vermillion, and that of its ruling principle is white.

3. The Manipuraka chakra is located at the solar plexus. Its ten petals have the color of the rain-cloud, and its ruling principles is fire.

4. The Anahata chakra lies in the spinal center that controls the heart region. It has twelve petals, its smoke-colored Mandala is six-pointed, forming the interlaced triangels, and represents the air element.

5. The Vishuddha chakra lies in the spinal area connected with the base of the throat. It has 16 petals, its color is grayish purple, and it represents the ether element.

6. The Ajna chakra is located in the spinal center of the region getween the eyebrows, at the thalamus, the sensory basal ganglion of the brain. It is lustrous moon-white in color, shining with a mystic trance-like beauty.

7. The Sahasrara chakra is situated in the crown of the head, "and is the dwelling place of Shiva." On its thousand petals are the letters of the Sanskrit

alphabet twenty times.

Marriage of the Lamb

In the Sahasrara chakra the Female Creative Principle meets and unites with its opposite princeiple (Shiva, positive, masculine) after its ascent from the Life Center at the base of the spine up thru the various chakras.

Here there is revealed in the Hindu Scroll that mysterious marriage of the Lamb, which is falsely represented to the Christian world as meaning the marriage of the gospel Jesus to the Roman Catholic Church.

Kundalini Power

1. When the Yogin opens the Earth Chakra by the rising power of the Kundalini, he conquers the earth. and no earthly element can injure him.

2. Next, the Yogin moves the Kundalini power up to the second chakra, the Water Chakra. By activating this chakra the Yogin is free from all sorrow; no water can harm him. He may be thrown in the deepest water, but "he will never die in the water."

3. As the Kundalini power moves up. it activates the Fire Chakra. Then "fire can not harm or burn the Yogin."

4. The next is the Air Chakra. When it is activated, the Yogin has mastered levitation, and he will never be disturbed by air.

5. Here the Kundalini flows upward and opens the Ether Chakra, the gate of liberation and emancipation. Then the Yogin can go wherever he likes, as swiftly as the Mind. "Behld, I come qucikly". (Rev. 3:11; 22:7, 12, 20).

6. When the Kundalini Power opens the Ajna chakra, at the thelamus, the sensory basal ganglion of the brain, the Yogi controls all the finer forces of nature and mental knowledge. He rises above nature's elements and is one with Atma. His mind is listening to the inner sound of the Nada,—it is the blessed joy that can be known only by one who has attained that state.

7. When the Kundalini Power opens the Sahasrara chakra, the Yogi cannot be bound in any of the three worlds. He can flash thru the sky at will with the speed of the Mind.

"The Sadhaka who has known the Great Void in the Sahasrara is freed from rebirths (reincarnation)."

This was the ultimate goal of Initiation in the Ancient Mysteries, and is the sum and substance of the mysterious Hindu scroll.

The Seven Churches in Asia

According to the authorized version of Revelation, God gave it to Jesus Christ, and he sent it by his angel to his servant John, who passed it on "to the seven churches which are in Asia" (Rev. 1:1-4). More Fraud.

Asia Minor was the native land of Apollonius, therefore typifying the homeland of his Solar Body; and the Seven Societies, called churches in the authorized version, are designated by the names of Asian cities, each of which, by some well-known characteristic or something for which it was noted, calls to mind the somatic center of the body which it represents.

These cities are listed in the same order in the Apocalypse as are the chakras in the Upanishads, which is further evidence to prove that India was the source and origin of the Hindu scroll that became the last book of the Christian Bible, and that the cities represent the seven chakras of the body.

1. The Muladhara chakra, sacral nerve ganglion; Ephesos, a city celebrated in Bible times for its great temple of Diana (Acts 19: 24-35), the "many-breasted mother," who appears in the Apocalypse as the "Woman clothed with the Sun, the Moon underneath her feet," the lunar goddess, the Isis of Egypt, and the Apocalyptic heroine, alike all symbolizing the regenerative force, the Solar Fire of the body, the Kundalini Force, mystically called the World-Mother, the Mother of the Universe.

2. Swadhisthana chakra, prostatic nerve ganglion; Smyrna, noted for the fig industry...The fig is preeminently a phallic symbol. "And the eyes of them both were opened, and they knew they were naked; and they sewed fig leaves together, and made themselves aprons" (Gen. 3:7).

3. Manipuraka chakra, solar plexus nerve ganglion; Pergamos, celebrated for its temple of Aesculapius; the epigastric or solar plexus is the controlling center of the vital processes of the body, and of the forces utilized in all systems of psychic healing.

4. Anahata chakra, cardiac nerve ganglion; Thyateira, a city noted for the manufacture of scarlet dyes, the name being thus a covert reference to the blood and the circulatory system.

5. Vishaddhi chakra, laryngeal nerve ganglion; Sardeis a name which suggests the sardion, sardine, or carnelian, a flesh-colored stone, thus alluding to the laryngeal protuberance commonly called "Adam's apple."

6. Aja chakra, cavernous nerve ganglion; Philadelphia, a city which was repeatedly destroyed by earthquakes; representing the fact that the manifestation of the Solar Fire, the Kundalini Force, is especially violent at the sixth chakra. And so Apollonius describes the activation or opening of the sixth seal as being accompanied by a "great earthquake" (Rev. 6:12-17)

-24-

7. Sahasrara chakra, the conarium or pineal gland of the brein. the "third eye. " Laodikeie, noted for the manufacture of the so-called "Phrygien powder," which was esteemed a soveriegn remedy for sore and weak eyes, presumably the "eyesalve" mentioned by Apollonius in the message to this seventh Society (Rev. 3:18).

To each of these Seven Societies (chakras) a message is sent; and in these messages the nature and function of each chakre is indicated. A particular aspect of the Solar Fires is presented to each one, a good and a bad quality being ascribed to each chakra, and a reward or prize is promised, specifying the astral results accruing to "the Conqueror" from the conquest (activation) of each chakra.

All of which refers to nothing but man's body, and the seven major nerve gnanglia therof.

CHAPTER NO. III

ENDOCRINE SYSTEM

Biblical symbols end parables deal with man, not with God and heaven es taught by the church.

In man's own body must we search for the secrets concealed in these symbols and parables; and their interpretation involves a profound knowledge of the mysterious ductless glands of the body and their functions.

The Ancient Masters who wrote the ancient literature were not the superstitious, idolatrous heathens that have been pictured to the modern world.

These men were scientists of the first order, and their symbols end parables conceal certain facts that they discovered as to the psycho-bio-physiology of the human body.

Medical art knows so little as to the various departments of the body and their functions, that when it first found the ductless glands not long ego, these glands were regarded as "hang-over appandages from the ape days of man," and no longer useful to him.

So the doctors began cutting them out end casting them into the garbege can. As their victims lived just as long as it took them to die from this ruthless, ignorant work, medical art took another look end decided thet the endocrine system of glands must be of some special use to the body.

The press of October 27, 1936, stated that Dr. Hans Lisser, "distinguished clinical professor of medicine at the University of California medical school," had listed "five modern miracles accomplished by endocrinology—the study of the ductless glands."

"Modernmiracles" are now "accomplished by endocrinology" in the life of man, whereas only twenty-five years ago so little was taught by medical art of these same glands, that they were cut out and thrown away.

Some of these "miracles" are mentioned by Lisser, and we shall quote what he said about the efffect of these glands on the sexual centers:

"For years the medical world was puzzled by such cases as this: A woman, say 30 years old who perhaps had borne children, would suddenly begin to turn into a man. She would grow a beard, her breasts would wither, her voice deepen, and she would present other attribute of a man.

"Through the learning of endocrinology, it is now possible to refeminitize such a woman.

"This may be done if we are able to locate and remove a tumor of the adrenal glands, or a certain type of ovarian tumor, or a lesion of the pituitary gland (of the brain).

"Every woman possesses masculine qualities or potentialities (and every man possesses feminine qualities or potentialities).

"Every man has a certain number of sex hormones in his blood, and vice-versa.

"When the male hormones predominate, we have a man; and when there is an excessive number of female hormones, we have a rather effeminate man. And because there are too many male hormones present, we have some virile, aggressive women.

"When a tumor appears on one of the glands mentioned, the excretion of female hormones is retarded; and male qualities begin to predominate. By removing the tumor, we return the woman to her normal balance."

If the small things mentioned will produced such marked changes in man and woman, what are the changes that will appear when such vital glands as the pituitary and pineal of the brain, semi-dormant in most people, are aroused, resurrected, and activated to the point when they function as they should?

Keep these facts in mind as we go along, for we are now at the threshold of the top secret of the Ancient Masters in the discovery, development and activation of the sixth and seventh sense powers of the body.

The god of the Masters was the Seven Sense Powered Man, and the heaven of the Masters was the Mind of that Man. For that was the Kingdom of the God within (Lu. 17:21), and that Man knew all things. From that Man "There is nothing covered, that shall not be revealed; and nothing hid, that shall not be known" (Mat. 10:26).

Compared with the Ancient Masters, modern science is in only the most primary stages of its work regarding the mysterious ductless glands.

Because of the great and peculiar part they plan in Man's development, and the general ignorance of medical art as to their functions, it is highly important to discuss these strange glands somewhat in detail.

That marvellous communication system of the Homo Sapiens, often termed the Brain System of Man,--what do the scientists really know about it? They do not even agree as to whether or not it is confined only to the Brain System. They cannot even agree as to just what constitutes the Brain System.

The great Carrel declares that "each man is far larger and more diffused then his body.... Man diffuses thru space in a positive way. In telepathic phenomena, he instantaneously sends out a part of himself, a sort of emanation, which joins a far-away relative or friend. He thus expands to great distances, He may cross oceans and continents in a time too short to be estimated" (Man The Unknown, pp. 258, 259, 260).

THE SEVEN CHAKRAS

It is unnecessary for the purpose here to dip deeply into the ductless gland system, but it is well to show the relationship of the Seven Chakras.

1. The Pineal gland, located in the roof of the third ventricle of the brain, is often mentioned as the Cyclops or Third Eye.

Cyclops was a fabulous race of giants having but one eye, in the center of the forehead.

Science terms this gland an atrophied third eye because in most men it is dormant, and its functions are unknown to science. And this is the seat of man's seventh sense power of consciousness.

The vibratory rate of the force emanations of this gland is so rapid as to be beyond any rate of vibration capable of being registered by any instruments so far produced, and has been estimated to be in the billions of cycles per second.

The Pineal is also the Sahasrara chakra, in the inner center of which "is the Great Void worshipped by the Devas in secret.... The Sadheka who has known the Great Void in the Sahasrara is freed from rebirths (reincarnation). He can not be bound in any of the three worlds, and can travel the sky at will" (Kundalini Power).

The effects on body and mind of the resurrection and activation of this chakra are described in symbol and parable in chapters 8, 9, 10 and 11 of Revelation.

2. The Pituitary gland occupies the sella turcica of the sphenoid bone, and the third ventricle of the brain extends into the stem (infundibulum) and the rear part of this gland. The rear part is said to be the seat of Solar Man, and the front part the seat of the Psychic Body which controls the involuntary functions of the body (p. 959).

The gland has two lobes, the anterior lobe regulating growth, especially of the bony structure, and is closely associated with the genital organs. The posterior lobe regulated pituitin, contracts the muscles, raises blood pressure, increases urine flow. excretion of milk, etc.

All these functions of the gland were well-known to the Ancient Masters, and in the Bible, 4th chapter of Zechariah, is an intersting fable relating to this gland, there symbolized as Zerubbabel, the builder of the temple (human body). What do the clergy know of these bio-physiological processes? Nothing.

The Pituitary gland is also the Ajna chakra, the spinal center for the region between the eyebrows. It is lustrous moon-white in color, shining with a mystic, trance-like beauty. The letters H and KSh are on its two petals. Its reigning tattva or elements; principle is mental function (manas). Within the trikona is the Itara Linga which is the Siva that enables one to rise above the element of Time.

Rishi Singh Gherwal writes: "The Ajna Chakra is the source of all Sidhis. Reaching here the Yogi controls all the finer forces of nature and mental knowledge. He rises above nature's elements and mind, and is one with Atma, above the world's miseries. His mind is listening to the inner sound of the Nada,--- it is the blessed joy that can be known by one only who has attained that state" (Kundalink, p. 78).

The effects on the body of the resurrection and activation of this chakra are described in symbol and allegory in the 9th, 10th, and 11th verses of chapter 6 of Revelation.

3. The Thyroid Gland, situated in the neck, regulates the production and distribution of thyroxin, a complex iodine compound. It is an important gland to the balanced function of the body, aiding digestion, elimination, etc.

4. The Parathyroid Gland is embedded in the Thyroid and regulates metabolism, calcium salts, lactic acid, phosphates and prophylactics necessary to maintain a balanced condition of the body, and it plays an important part in brain, nerve and sex function.

The Laryngeal, Pharyngeal, Thyroid and Parathyroid regions are ruled by the Vishuddha Chakra, which is the highest of those belonging strictly to the sympathetic system, the ones above it being in the brain.

Ether is the element of this chakra, and is indicated in Yoga literature by a large white or colorless circle.

The effects on the body of the resurrection and activation of this chakra are described in symbol and allegory in verse 8, chapter 6, of Revelation.

5. The Thymus Gland extends from the throat down to the heart and medical art believes the gland should gradually disappear as the genital organs develop. Like most medical theories, this one is questioned, as there is still a trace of

the gland all thru life, showing some activity.

It is true that this gland, as now known, is largest and most active during childhood, but it functions in adult age. And when we consider that it does not appear logical for any gland in the body to atrophy and shrink in size without a definite cause, we should regard this condition of the Thymus as being unnatural and the result of some bad habit. It means little that medical art does not so regard it.

PARTHENOGENESIS

In our work titled "The Great Red Dragon" we stated that many ages have passed since parthenogenesis was the regular order of human propagation; but some clues still remain which appear to show the reason why sexual generation succeeded asexual generation (virgin birth).

Between the ages of puberty and the menopause, it is usual now for women to expel from each ovary in turn, at monthy intervals, matured ova. This process is termed ovulation, and appears responsible for menstruation.

Ovulation consists in the enlargement of the Graafian Follicle of the ovary. The enlargement protrudes in the form of a sac filled with fluid and an ovum. Finally the sac bursts, and the fluid and ovum pass on to the uterus, and, if fertilized by the male element, the ovum adheres to the uterine wall and develops into an embryo. Otherwise it perishes and passes off.

Some biologists hold that the process of ovulation, like menstruation, appears abnormal. It is not usual in lower animals, and no reason appears why woman should be an exception to the rule.

This periodic rupture of the ovaries, accompanied by pain and a discharge of vital fluid from the uterus, devitalizes and deteriorates the body, making auto-impregnation impossible.

In a girl, before menstruation begins, the vestigial male sex organs in her body are still capable of functioning.

Here appears the point in woman's development where the Thymus is involved. This organ is termed "the gland of youth". It is most active at puberty; and then, for some unknown reason, it begins to atrophy slowly, and, as a rule, becomes quite inactive after maturity, with premature decrepitude often following.

Experiments show that the Thymus acts as a "check valve" on the gonads. When the Thymus is removed in rats, the result is greater sexual activity, greater propagation, faster deterioration, and shorter life. This fact seems to reveal another reason why man is in a serious state of degeneration.

Deterioration and atrophy of the Thymus seems to produce the change of puberty, resulting in the atrophy of the male qualities in the female, and leading to the excessive development of the female characteristics at the expense of the male qualities.

The bisexuality of embryonic life disappears, being succeeded by an abnormal degree of either maleness or femaleness. This condition seems to result largely from the atrophy of the Thymus in the pre-pubescent child.

In childhood, the Thymus is developed and functional. So it must have been in the early ancestors of the race before degeneration set in; and the bisexual state of the creative organs did not then deteriorate, and bisexuality must have been the general condition, with auto-impregnation by psychic power the rule, and man was virgin born.

So says the ancient tradition, and so we have shown in our work titled "The Virgin Birth Debate."

Biologists hold that when atrophy of the Thymus first began, females first appeared as the first step in the degenerative course.

This may be an answer to the strange statement in the Bible, "That the sons of God (bisexual creative units) saw the daughters of men (first females who appeared as the first step in degeneration) that they were fair; and they took them wives of all which they chose" (Gen. 6:2).

The manner in which this event is mentioned indicates that it was an unusual occurence; something out of the ordinary and not regular.

"By the process of modification it is possible to produce new varieties" said Darwin, and a case of that modification seems to face us here.

Leading scientists hold that woman carried the race on for long ages, as we have shown in "The Virgin Birth Debate," before the next step in degeneration weakened her bisexual qualities and led to the appearance of uni-sexuality.

This cosmic condition is still recapitulated in the embryo. As the infant begins to develop, its sex largely depends on the Thymus, with slight deterioration of the gland resulting in a girl, and greater deterioration resulting in a boy, according to biologists.

The reason why the Thymus atrophies is a mystery to science, but not to naturists and hygienists, and not to the great Carrel, who wrote: "How can we prevent the degeneracy of man in modern civilization" (Man The Unknown, p. 5).

Civilized man lives an artificial life in an environment where there is everything imaginable which produces his degeneration. But industrialism and commercialism come first, and man's improvement never if it interferes with the money making processes.

We are told that in the early days when primitive man lived a more natural life, there was no atrophy of the Thymus, and there should be none now.

The Thymus regulates and compounding of the glandular substances, controls heart action and the sensations in the heart area. For instance, we do not love with all our heart, but with all our Thymus.

When we experience joy or fright, and feel that strange sensation in the heart region, we think it is the heart, whereas it is the action of the Thymus.

This region of the body is ruled by the Anahata Chakra, which lies in the spinal center of the heart area. Its smoke-colored mandale is six-pointed, forming the interlaced triangles, and stands for the air element.

The effects of the resurrection and activation of this chakra is described in symbol and allegory in verses 5 and 6 of the 6th chapter of Revelation.

6. The Spleen, not considered by some as a ductless gland, is situated in the left upper quadrant of the abdomen. It is one of the most important filtration stations of the body, and operates under the vibratory of the Pituitary gland, "the builder of the temple," in combination with the Parathyroid, forming an operating Triad.

7. The Suprarenals, a duo gland situated just above the kidneys, the central portion of which regulates adrenalin, the activating fluid of the body, preparing man to flee or fight in case of danger. Fright, anger, and many forms of shock cause excess quantitites of adrenalin to be excreted into the blood by these glands.

8. The Pancreas is situated in the back of the upper part of the abdomen. It regulates insulin, sugar, starch, alcoholic toxins, etc. It also receives and precipitates minute quantities of nitron gas from sunlight or atmospheric gases that have been exposed to sunlight.

These glands are ruled by the Manipuraka Chakra, located in the solar plexus, and its ruling principle is Fire. "When the Yogin opens this chakra, known as the Fire Dharana, the killer of the fear of death, then 'fire cannot harm nor burn the Yogin'" (Kundalini, p. 44).

The effects on the body of the resurrection and activation of this chakra are described in symbol and allegory in verse 4 of the 6th chapter of Revelation.

9. The Prostate Gland is not listed as one of the endocrine system, but we shall list it here because of its importance in this work. It lies near the base of the back-bone and is larger than a hen's egg. It contacts the lower part of the bladder, and thru it the urethra passes as it leaves the bladder.

Science knows little about this gland, its functions, or the purpose of its excretions. More will be said on this later (p. 214).

10. The Gonads (sex glands) regulate the centers of propagation, glycogen, and lactic acid. And it should be noted under Radiation that lactic acid and glycogen are two of the few elements that stimulate and activate the brain cells —which indicate that the proper function of the brain cells depends on

the Gonads. So the brain cells must suffer if the product of the Gonalds is diss-
ipeted in any way.

The Prostate and Gonads are fuled by the Svadhishthana and Muladhara
chakras. The ruling principle of the former is water, and that of the latter is
the earth or solid matter.

The effects on the body of the resurrection and activation of these chakras
are described in symbol and allegory in verses 2 and 12-17 of the 6th chapter of
Revelation.

SOLOMON'S TEMPLE

In the Bible his name is Solomon. In the Greek it was Shelomeh.

The Bible states that he built a temple "which is overlaid with pure gold"
(2 Chr. 3:4, 5). The Ancient Masters considered gold condensed solar rays.

This Temple symbolized the human body. Its construction required 13
years (1 K. 5:5; 7:1),--which represents the 12 signs of the Zodiac and the Sun
in the center, making 13.

Jesus had 12 disciples, which represented the 12 signs of the Zodiac, and
he represented the Sun, making 13.

This Temple was a school of the Ancient Mysteries. On the wall was a
chart of the Endocrine Glands, showing what modern science has only recently
discovered.

To be admitted to this school, the candidate had to prove by proper test
that he was worthy of acceptance. Here he was taught the mysteries of Live,
and in correct, though mystic terms, the facts of mind power now recognized
as psychology. He was also taught that the universe is a sequence of synth-
etic action, of constant change, a chemical process of creative evolution and
involution,--of unfolding from the invisible to the visible, and of infolding
from the visible to the invisible,--the cosmic cycle of transformation.

THE FOUR BEASTS

The Four Beasts so often mentioned in the Bible constitute the ancient
Sphinx, as explained in our work of that title.

In the biblical fables these Beasts play their part in the various dramas,
the best and most complete of which is the Apocalyptic drama.

I saw, when the Lamb opened one of the seven seals, and I heard one of
the four Beasts saying as with a voice of thunder, Come and see (Rev. 6:1).

We saw in the chakras listed above, that the Muladhara represents the
earth: the Svadhishthana represents water, the Manipura represents Fire and

the Anahata represents Fire, and the Anahata represents air.

In "THE MYSTERIOUS SPHINX" we said: "The church fathers were careful to conceal the fact that the Sphinx, The Four Fixed Signs of the Zodiac, and the Great Pyramid symbolize the Four Cosmic Principles which constitute man, as follows:
1. Solar Radiation is the Spark of Life;
2. Air is the Breath of Life;
3. Water is the River of Life;
4. Dust of the Earth is the Body of Life."

The Sphinx was hoary with age before the books of the Bible were ever written, yet is never mentioned in the Bible except in the wildest terms.

Ezekiel saw a whirlwind come out of the north, a great cloud, and a fire infolding itself.....and out of the midst thereof came the likeness of four living creatures.

Then the biblical makers proceeded to give a sensational description of the Sphinx, and mixed it up with the Zodiac, the description of which is just as sensational (Chap. 1:4, 5, 15-21).

Daniel saw strange things in a vision. The four winds of heaven arrove upon the great sea (Mediterranean), and four great beasts (Sphinx) came up from the sea. Then follows another sensational description of the Sphinx.

In Revelation the same four beasts appear in the midst of the throne and round about the throne. Then follows another description of the Sphinx.

Why does the Sphinx seem to play such an important part in the ancient scriptures? Because these four Beasts (Beings) symbolize the Four Cosmic Elements which constitute man; and there is nothing at all mysterious about them when the hidden facts are uncovered and revealed.

The same is true of the entire Bible. The context is confusing and was purposely made so by the biblical makers, for the benefit of the church and the detriment of the masses.

The Bible is the greatest book of distortion, interpolation, fraud, falsehood and misrepresentation that man has ever produced, and the whole purpose of the work was the enslavement of humanity.

No system of enslavement which the world has ever known, has been so clever and so complete as that termed Roman Catholicism.

CHAPTER 4

FIERY SERPENT & FALSE PROPHET

Cosmic Forces work like a double-edged sword, cutting for Good in one direction and for Evil in the other, the result depending upon the use of the force.

The Key to the Secret of Life, opined the Ancient Masters, lay in the Creative Function of the organism. Where else could it be?

The Masters saw that dual forces, two creative principles, were everywhere combined in creative or transformative processes. These forces they symbolized in the Caduceus as the White and Black Serpents, explained in our work titled "The Magic Wand".

The White Serpent represented the active, positive, masculine principle, and the Black represented the passive, negative, feminine principle. These are the two edges of the sword.

With the Masters, a study of the Creative Force of the body was scientific in intent and far removed from thoughts of things unclean and obscene.

To the Masters, in their purity of mind, the most sacred and vital part of man is that possessing the mysterious power of procreation.

For in possessing that power, man is a creator in his own right. He is a free agent, an independent being, and is responsible for his own deportment. He has within himself the power of perpetuity, and can never become extinct. He has within himself all the potentialities of his own existence. He is the God of his universe.

In all ancient religions, the deepest and most awe-inspiring attribute in Nature, is the power of procreation. Nature holds no greater secret than the mystery of propagation, the creation of man, and creation by man.

This deepest riddle of Life has attracted in every age of the past the thoughts and attention of the world's greatest philosophers and scientists.

The Masters studied man as a creative being. They considered every part and particle of the body involved in creative work; and discovered strange secrets of life which they did not dare to impart to the masses, but entrusted them only to their disciples, who proved by rigid test that they were worthy to receive the knowledge.

These secrets were never committed to writing, except in heavily veiled symbol and allegory that could be understood only by the initiate. Hence, for the exoteric the Bible is a book of confusion.

The scriptures of the Masters contained dual and triple messages, cleverly formulated to mislead the exoteric, while teaching the esoteric the profound mysteries of Life.

A typical example of this appears in the following allegory that refers to the Serpentine Fire:

-34-

Make thee a Fiery Serpent, and set it upon a pole; and it shall come to pass, that everyone that is bitten, when he looketh upon it, shall live" (Num. 21:8).

To him who has the key, it is clear to what the allegory refers.

The Serpentine Force is the Solar Fire of the body, as many testify, making the ancient symbol perfectly plain, and constraining Paul to say, "It is better to marry than to burn" (1 Cor. 7:8, 9).

The word "bitten" is well used. It means the act of copulation. The term "shall live" implies that those who gaze at the symbol will be constrained to remember what they did, and cause them to think of the serious consequences of the act, and to strive to live a better life.

Confusing parables relating to this vital subject run all thru the Bible, the best ones appearing in Genesis, Ezekiel, Isaiah, Haggi, Zecharian, New Testament and Revelation.

Taken literally, biblical parables confuse, mislead, fail to make sense. That was intended. Taken symbolically, the literature in the Bible is the best the world has, — but only on one vital subject; and that subject is related to the Edenic Parable and to him that overcometh the temptations of the flesh, and obeyeth the command not to eat of the "forbidden fruit."

To that one vital subject refer all the teachings contained in the ancient scriptures.

The first lesson one should learn is that the teachings of the Bible deal with one subject, tell one story, and tell it in many ways. It deals always with Man in relation to his Creative Powers, causing some scholars to term the Bible a book of Phallic Worship.

The tale begins with the Talking Serpent in Genesis, and closes with the Great Red Dragon in Revelation.

The characters in the parables represent cosmic principles, cosmic elements, cosmic processes, involving secret processes of the body not as yet discovered by modern science.

It may seem strange that these things are often represented by the Serpent. The Masters considered the Serpent the best and most fitting of all symbols.

The Serpent plays two parts, presenting the Two Cosmic Principles of Creation. One is the Good Serpent, the other is the Bad Serpent. The Former is the White Serpent of the Caduceus, and represents the positive power of the creative processes. The latter is the Black Serpent, and represents the negative power of the creative processes.

It is the Black Serpent that appears in the Edenic parable and beguiles woman.

It represents the Pituitary gland of the brain called in the Bible Zarubbabel, "the builder of the temple" (human body) (Zech. 49). In Revelation it appears as the Great Red Dragon (Rev. 12), -- one of the strongest forces in life.

The Black Serpent is also the False Prophet, and symbolizes Sex Force in creative action. It deceives its victims by yielding pleasure while destroying body and mind. That made it the chief target of attack by the Masters. To save the race, it must be conquered and controlled. All will agree who read our work titled "The Great Red Dragon."

THE ANCIENT WARNING

The famous Edenic parable warns humanity to reject the False Prophet, or suffer the sad consequences. The warning was addressed to woman, for on her directly and ultimately depends propagation.

The Masters based the parable on their wide knowledge of the strange functions of the mysterious ductless glands, and especially, in this case, on the Pituitary.

Modern science has recently discovered what the Masters had known for thousands of years,--that this gland is a veritable control center of the body, pouring into the blood no less than six powerful hormones, which exert dictatorial power over the entire endocrine system.

The entire book of Zechariah refers to the various angles of this subject, and many identical features are mentioned that appear in Revelation, such as the measurement of the city, the various colored horses, and other things.

This potent force of the Pituitary in woman, in the department of pro-creation, must be subdued and controlled in order for man to move up to the higher life.

Propagation pulls man down to the animal level. The generative function is strictly nothing but an animal one, and can never be anything else. Higher thoughts produce higher results only thru higher acts. Thus taught the Masters.

True spirituality demands the utter extirpation of the procreative function. While its proper exercise for the continuation of the race, in the semi-animal stage, may not be considered unlawful, its misuse, in any way, is fraught with the most terrible consequences physically, and spiritually.

Another secret of the Masters, unknown to modern science, is the reason why woman is more "psychic" than man. The Pituitary, organ of the sixth sense, is more active in woman than in man--due largely to the fact that it governs the procreation centers, and woman is the producer.

WOMAN WAS WARNED

The Microcosm is the product of the Macrocosm. The so-called mother is not the actual producer. She is the medium thru which the Macrocosm produces; and she is that medium only so long as she maintains sufficient quality. And as she bears, she deteriorates.

Production is the means to an end, exactly as the Masters taught. In the day that thou eatest of the "forbidden fruit", dying thou shalt die.

Creative Law, acting directly on woman, activates the Pituitary, giving her greater psychic power, and causing her, in her present unisexual state, to seek the male for help, that she may fulfill the command, "Be fruitful and multiply" (Gen. 1:28).

A command is not a law, and may be broken without damaging results, as we have stated in The Great Red Dragon (p. 6).

And in this particular case, the commandment is followed by another, which appears to nullify the first; for it informs man that if he did eat of the "forbidden fruit", the result would be degeneration and early death (Gen. 2:17).

To put greater emphasis upon this commandment, the Masters warned woman that if she yielded to the creative urge, it would---

"Greatly multiply thy sorrow and thy conception; in sorrow thou shalt bring forth children; and thy desire shall be to thy husband, and he shall rule over thee" (Gen. 2:16).

Then the Masters cautioned man to help woman by not yielding to her influence. Man ignored the caution; and so---

"Because thou hast harkened unto the voice of thy wife, and hast eaten of the tree, of which we commanded thee, saying, Thou Shalt not eat of it; cursed is the ground for thy sake; in sorrow shalt thou eat of it all the days of thy life; thorns also and thistles shall it bring forth to thee" (Gen. 3:16-18).

Now if this is the "Fall of Man", surely the remedy offered by the church is not the answer.

For man reaps as he sows (Ga. 6:7). He alone must correct his errors, and suffer for them. That penalty cannot be put on the back of a mythical savior.

HUMAN LIFE CHEAP

Down thru the ages, despots and tyrants have opposed all teachings that lead man up to a better life.

The Edenic warning of the Masters is utterly ignored by the church, by all governments, and by the social pattern. Propagation is promoted to supply the dictators with slaves and soldiers.

Some governments promote production by payment of premiums to women who the biggest family. According to this rule, she who produces no progeny is a failure.

Nothing is cheaper than human life. The general of an army thinks less of sacrificing (expending) soldiers to gain his objective, than he does of the dust on his boots. He is proud of his victories, and eater to expend more soldiers to gain more "glory".

So despots and tyrants oppose the teachings that benefit man, and murder the Masters to still their voices.

The Masters were forced to go "underground" and to conceal their secrets in symbol and allegory in order to preserve them.

Had the biblical makers known that the secret of redemption is concealed in symbol and allegory in Revelation, that book had never been included in the Bible. Even then it was not included until it had been greatly distorted by a clever priest.

A COSMIC PRINCIPLE

Chapter 15 of 1st Corinthians is headed "Of Christ's Resurrection". Every word and every line of reference to "Christ" is that chapter is a spurious interpolation, being the work of the clever priest.

Paul (Pol) referred not to a person, but to a Cosmic Principle. He had mentioned fornication, called it "sin", and was discussing the super-refined Life Essence of the Gonad glands, which the Greeks termed "Chrisma" and which is the expended and dissipated in copulation.

"Every sin that a man doeth is without the body; but he that committeth fornication sinneth against his own body;... for the wages of sin is death" (Rom. 6:18; 1 Cor. 6:18).

Thus we behold how greatly the biblical makers distorted the ancient scriptures, and then destroyed them. Not a scroll can be found from which the Bible was made. When a new discovery is made of an ancient scroll, the church is frightened, and the church authorities rush in and take charge of it.

By conservation of the Life Essence, man is able to increase the Cosmic Fire within his own body, where it becomes as a Flame which burns, yet does not consume, as symbolized by the Burning Bush which Moses saw (Ex. 3:2).

The Serpentine Fire ceases to burn when raied up to the Brain, the Throne of the Most High, the Seat of all knowledge and all humanistic power (Ps. 91:1).

And that was the subject which Paul (Pol) discussed in the 15th chapter of 1st Corinthians.

When the Serpentine Fire is raised up to the Brain and has opened the Seven

-38-

Seals of the body (Book--Rev. 5), it then becomes the Great Fruit of Man
(1 cor. 15:20).

Such Man has overcome the temptation of the flesh, has obeyed the command
not to eat of the "forbidden fruit", and he inherits all things good in life, and I
(Perfection) will be his Guide, and he shall be my Son (Rev. 21:7).

The Serpentine Fire resurrects and activates the Pituitary and Pineal glands
of the brain, the organs of the Sixth and Seventh Senses, and produces the strange
powers of clairaudience and clairvoyance, the powers of the Seer.

The Greek copy of the Bible said: "THE EVIDENCE OF SUCH RESURRECTION
IS THE POWER OF SEERSHIP."

In the authorized version it reads: "THE TESTIMONY OF JESUS IS THE SPIRIT
OF PROPHECY" (Rev. 19:10).

That is a typical example of the manner in which the ancient scriptures were
distorted and interpolated by the biblical makers.

When the Sixth and Seventh Senses are resurrected and activated, these
super-powers exalt man to the most high plane of super-consciousness, in which
he rises above the cosmic element of Space-Time and it disappears; the past-
future blends into the eternal present, and all things become known.

For the Seer there is nothing covered, that shall not be revealed; and nothing hid, that shall not be known (Mat. 10:26).

LAW OF COMPENSATION

The Sacred Ark of the Covenant is another ancient symbol. Man is that
Sacred Ark, with the eternal Covenant written in his Brain,--that Covenant in-
volving the Redemption of Man from the evil of the accursed function of Sexual
Propagation.

For in the day that thou eatest of the "forbidden fruit," dying thou shalt
surely die (Gen. 2:17).

For as we procreate sexually, we degenerate physically. Production of the
New is the sacrifice of the Old.

As we consume the Solar Essence in creative action, we weaken body and
brain in compensation. As we sacrifice by producing, so we redeem by abstaining.

The Law of Compensation demands a sacrifice for every gain, and bestows
a regard for every self-denial. So the Masters wisely taught the doctrine of
self-denial. For Self-Denial in all things leads of health, happiness, and
longevity (Mat. 16:24, etc.)

-39-

By denying himself the fruit and the pleasure of sexual propagation. Man gains in every part of his body and brain. These blessings he sacrifices as he consumes his Solar Essence in propagation and pleasure.

On this subject one should read our work titled "The Great Red Dragon" (Rev. 12), the terrible beast that represents carnal lust, which may be devouring you by inches, and sapping your vitality, shortening your life, and forcing you into obscurity.

In his letter a reader asks us to explain how man can rise to the plane of Cosmic Consciousness. That is exactly what we are doing by giving the world the Lost Wisdom on the Ancient Masters.

Man rises to the plane of Cosmic Consciousness by stimulating and activating his dormant sense glands, and self denial is the path to the goal. Such man then possesses the "uncanny powers" of those wild Indians of South American mentioned in our work titled "Kingdom of Heaven" (p. 19).

THE BURNING BUSH

All of the biblical fables are related, and all of them deal with the creative powers of man. One of these fables is the Burning Bush.

The angel of the Lord (man's mind power) appeared unto Moses in a flame of fire, out of the midst of a bush; and the bush burned with fire, but was not consumed (Ex. 3:1-4).

The Tree in the midst of the Garden, the burning bush, the fiery serpent, and the Great Red Dragon (Rev. 12) are all related symbology.

At the base of the spine is the seat of the Fire of Life, the Creative Fire of the Microcosm that burns but does not consume--immediately.

The Creative Fire consumes slowly, by inches, and commences its work when the child begins to masturbate. So the Great Red Dragon stands ever ready to devour the child as soon as born (Rev. 12:4).

In October-1956 the press contained a picture of a young woman in South America, age 21, and her son of 16, born when she was only five.

No wonder the race degenerates. That is the real battle of Armagedoon that runs thru all the biblical fables.

That is the symbolism of the Burning Bush, where Moses represents humanity and the angel represents Mind, Ego, Consciousness, the Real Man.

The Tree of Life represents man's Spinal Cord, whose Living Sap is a creatove force.--a Fire than burns but consumes not.

Far from complete would Man be without the creative power. It represents the Great Tempation. or the great blessing. For this power can drag man down until he is lower than the beast, or exalt him to the sky.

Man must prove his ability to use this cosmic power wisely and well, or learn thru its misuse the hard lesson gained in the suffering of sad experience.

The high importance of the subject is the reason why the Bible is filled with teachings on Phallicism; and why such teachings were always held most sacred. They were always veiled from the masses in general, being revealed only to those whose purity of mind permitted them to grasp and appreciate the deeper truths of the teachings.

The Creative Power of Man is considered impure and unholy by the masses only because the social pattern and the conformists have so decreed it.

Ignorant leaders and their followers know not that a church steeple represents the phallus (male organ of generation), and the arch doors and windows of churches represent the cunnus (female organ of generation).

They know not that there can be no Redemption of Man, and no religious teachings of any value, which do not recognize the body's creative powers, and which are not based upon absolute purity of body and mind. The more esoteric the teachings, the more rigid the standard of purity.

When the Creative Fires of the Tree of Life are conserved. and have passed up thru the Spinal cord, opened the Seven Seals of the body (Rev. 5), and activated the Pineal gland of the brain (All-Seeing Eye), the Single Eye that fills the body with Light (Mat. 2:66; Lu. 11:34), man is then raised up in consciousness to the point where he can see the Glory of the Lord of the Earth, and know that he is that Lord of the Earth.

The masses in general never know anthing else but the impure side of the Life Centers of the body, and modern theology is largely responsible for that,

The ideals of the masses have been so badly shattered by contact with the exoteric misconceptions of sex, that they have put all thought of it from them as sonething too vile for consideration, and thus remain in darkness as to the higher side of life.

The esoteric know, and the esoteric should be taught, that the Redemption of Man and the awakening of the Kingdom of Heaven within, depends upon the puriffcation and proper use of all functions of body and brain for the Glorification of Man, the God of the Earth.

The Burning Bush, the Tree of Life is the Tree of Suffering and Death until, by conscious power, the Fires of Life are raised up from the lower aspect of the Spinal Cord and made to function in the brain. Then instead of producing unwanted progeny, it produces that God of the Earth which Man was made to be (Gen. 1:28).

It is thru the terrible perversion of man's creative power that made it the great sin mentioned by Paul.

What fruit had ye then in those things (fornication) whereof ye are now ashamed." For the end of those things is death. The wages of sin (fornication) is death (Gen. 3:17; Rom. 6:21, 23).

The Pauline epistles contain frequent references to carnal lust and fornication.

In the 15th chapter of 1st Corinthians, falsely headed "Of Christ's Resurrection," Paul discussed the raising up to the brain of the Fires of Life also termed Kundalini. Insert the word Kundalini for Christ, and we see what Paul was discussing.

And if Kundalini be not raised, then is our preaching vain, and your faith isalso vain....And if Kundalini be not raised, your faith is vain; ye are yet in your sins (of fornication) ℟ Cor. 15:14, 17).

In their translation, the church fathers inserted many spurious interpolations in their scheme to make the reader believe Paul was talking about Christ.

Paul never heard of the gospel Jesus.

PAUL AND MARRIAGE

The 7th chapter of 1st Corinthians is headed "Sacredness of the marriage bond." What did Paul really think of marriage?

Paul observed the law that in the Resurrection (Regeneration), they neither marry, nor are given in marriage, but are as the angels (free of fornication) (Mat. 22:30).

Paul regarded marriage as bad, for it promotes fornication and propagation. He favored it only as the lesser of two evils. This is what he said:

"It is good for the unmarried and widows if they abide as I (single). But if they cannot contain (their sex urge). let them marry. For it is better to marry than to burn" (1 Cor. 7:8, 9).

In his great work titled "Sex and Sex Worship", O. A. Wall, M.D., Ph.G., Ph. M., quoted one Lucinda B. Chandler, "a would-be social reformer," as follows:

"When a woman has made this (marriage) agreement...she has made herself permanently...a legal prostitute till death or divorce dissolves the contract. I demand the immediate and unconditional abolition of this vilest system that ever cursed the earth. Marriage is legalized prostitution...The term marriage is more offensive than the terms rape, murder, or prostitution,

as it involves all of them...The wife is the most degraded of all prostitutes...
a forced prostitute....Popular prostitution, bad as it is, is not so bad as the
forced prostitution of marriage" (p. 173).

The first requirement of the candidate for initiation in the Sacred Ancient
Mysteries. was rigid subjugation of his animal nature. The Egyptian Sphinx
was the ancient symbol of this subjugation.

Then the Fiery Serpent, instead of being the False Prophet, becomes the
mysterious psycho-bio-physiological force that activates the Pituitary and
Pineal, and elevates man to a state of super-consciousness.

CHAPTER 5

REGENERATION

Ye which have followed me in the Regeneration...shall sit in the throne of
his glory (Mat. 19:28).

The weight of authority holds that Regeneration depends primarily upon a
rigid conservation of the Solar Fire, the Divine Essence, the Fluid of Life.

In 1897 Kenneth S. Guthrie, A. M.   published a book entitled "Regeneration",
in which he said: "This book is written for the following purposes:

1. "To show that the Doctrine of Regeneration, or Sexual Continence, is
only the application to Man of the universally recognized Laws of Biology, as
set forth by the most able and recent authorities.

2. "To show that Regeneration is, according to the facts taught by the most
recognized medical writers, a psycho-bio-physiological process normal in Man,
and that total Continence is possible and beneficial.

3. "To explain scientifically the methods to gain entire control of the Creative Function.

4. "To show that the New Testament enforces it so clearly, that language
could not be more emphatic; and that the early Fathers of Christianity, from the
beginning, taught Regeneration as the central content of their religion.

5. "To show the Rationality of Continence, and that Regeneration supplies
a universally possible Plan of Life, which alone makes life worth living. by
showing how one can earn and attain bodily health and vitality."

The only sin definitely defined in the Bible is the act of fornication, which
defiles the body.

If any man defile the Temple of Man, him shall the gods destroy, for the
Temple of Man is holy. which Temple ye are (1 Cor. 3:16. 17).

Let not sin (copulation) reign in your mortal body, that he should obey it in the lust thereof (Rom. 6:13).

What fruits had ye then in those things (copulation) whereof ye are now ashamed?--Rom. 6:21.

The carnal mind is enmity against cosmic law; for it is not subject to the law of the Universe, neither indeed can be, as it is the work of lust (Rom. 7:7).

For this is the Law, even your sanctification, that ye should abstain from fornication. That every one of you should know how to possess his (generative) vessel (organ) in sanctification and honor; not in the lust of concupiscence (1 Thes. 4:3, 4).

Likewise also the men, leaving the natural use of woman, burned in their lust one toward another; men with men working that which is unseemly, and receiving in themselves that just recompense of their error (Rom. 1:27).

For even the women did change the natural use into that which is against nature (Rom. 1:26).

"The body is an instrument, and, as it were, a garment or robe of Solar Man; and if by this latter it be given over to fornication, it becomes defiled" (Cyril of Jerusalem).

"By moving reason in yourself and by kindling the spark of good by your free-will, you made yourself as an eunuch and acquired such a habit of virtue that impulse to vice became, almost, an impossibility to you" (Gregory of Nazianzus).

Origen castrated himself in order to conquer carnal lust, and thereafter became the victim of malicious thrusts.

For there are some eunuchs which were so born from their mother's womb (men who remain virgins); and there are some eunuchs which were made eunuchs (castrated). He that is able to receive it, let him receive it (Mat. 19:12).

Hermas, in his Pastor, said: "I charge you to guard your chastity. All of you should remain stedfast, and be as children, without doing evil (fornication), and you will be more honored than all."

Suffer little children to come unto me, and forbid them not; for of such is the kingdom of heaven (where carnal lust is entirely absent) (Mk. 10:14).

"For this was that said, 'Unless ye be converted, and become as children pure in flesh and holy in soul by abstinence from carnal lust.'"--Clement of Alexandria.

"To habe guarded one's purity from the womb, and to have kept oneself a child even to old age, throughout the whole life, is the part of the highest virtue" (Hippolytos).

"Angels walking upon earth are they who practice chastity. Let us not, for a brief pleasure, defile so great, so noble a body; for short and momentary is the sin. but the effect of the same endureth forever" (Cyril of Jerusalem).

"That we may become a new, holy people by Regeneration, and keep the men undefiled by the sin of fornication" (Clement of Alexandria).

The Bible teacnes implicitly that virginity is the only path thru which Regeneration is attainable. For all other paths to Regeneration lead to this one either directly or indirectly.

Virginity was the doctrine of all ancient religions; and the conception of priesthood and seership is so inseparably bound to that of Virginity, that all ancient temples required Virginity of their priests.

"And unto this gate (of the Eleusinian Mysteries) no unclean person shall enter, nor one that is carnal; as it is reserved for the chaste and pure only."

Hippolytos said that in the Eleusinian Mysteries there was no need of being emasculated (Castrated), but by being made a eunuch by means of hemlock, and despising carnal generation.

As to the Mysteries of Cybele, the Great Mother, we are told that "with the utmost severity and vigilance, they were enjoined to abstain from indulgence with woman, as tho they (men) were emasculated."

"What is more honorable that chastity, which makes of man an angel,"-- Bernard.

"To be and become a virgin is the result of virtue. It is not an earthly, BUT A DIVINE LIFE TO LIVE IN THE FLESH BEYOND THE FLESH; to live in the world and be not of the world."--Crysologos.

"As the angels neither marry nor are given in marriage (Mat. 22:30), and are not multiplied by the agency of flesh and blood, it is evident that they do not commingle on earth, and are not obnoxious due to envy and lust; are not in need of food or drink; and are not liable to be tempted" (Crysostom).

"Man alone is the image of Perfection when he does not perform actions similar to those of animals, but advances far beyond mere Humanity to the point of Divinity within him thru the power of Virginity."--Titian.

The principle doctrine of the Anti-Nicene Soteriology (Science of Health) centered in the Regeneration of Man by abstaining from carnal lust. But this doctrine were rejected by Sonstantine, who ruled the Nicene Council.

Baptism by Fire, to which men submitted when initiated in a certain ancient religious order, meant incineration with a red-hot iron of the testes, to insure Virginity.

-45-

But this operation, like castration, is degenerative, for it deprives the body of that precious Solar Quintessence, which is refined, elaborated and excreted by the important Gonad Glands.

Besides being the hidden secret of greatness of the Masters, Virginity was the source of the intelligence, power and originality manifested in the lives of the great mystics, like Apollonius, Tauler, Fenelon, Theresa, Swedenborg, etc.

History in general supports the contention that whenever unusual understanding, intelligence and originality appear in man, the basis of it is Virginity.

This was the secret of the remarkable success and vitality of the Ancient Mystery Schools, and the basic cause of their destruction, the final step of which destruction began in the fourth century when Constantine founded the Roman State Church.

SEERSHIP

Cosmic Intelligence produces an immense pressure in the creative centers of the body in order to attain certain purposes.

Without this immense flow of solar force into the creative centers, the original purpose of Life would probably not be attained, and Cosmic Intelligence would fail to make man serve the law of production.

The guarantee against this is the immense pressure in the creative centers which rules man, blinds him, make him a servant, forces him to serve the law of production, in the belief that he has no higher purpose in life than that of serving himself, gratifying his passions, and satisfying his desires.

Apart from the obvious purpose of propagation, sex power serves another purpose in the life of man. The existence of this additional purpose explains the reason why sexual force is generated in such quantity, and directed to the creative centers.

One of these purposes is to perpetuate the race. The other, the higher, the more deeply hidden, is the development of man's brain in the acquisition of a state of consciousness far above the animal level, which is secured by the resurrection and activation of man's latent forces and faculties.

It is the express explanation of this latter, higher purpose that forms the whole content and meaning to all esoteric teachings, and was the sole subject of the ancient scriptures.

It required much distortion and clever interpolation on the part of the biblical makers to conceal that subject, and to over-shadow it with a new doctrine, invented by the church, in the form of a mysterious heaven, an anthropomorphic God. and a "savior" of race.

This higher, deeply hidden purpose differs from the first in that it is not automatic, and requires conscious effort on the part of man himself, and a definite orientation of his whole life.

However, the rule that this higher purpose is not automatic applies to civilized man, to man living in that state of artificialism erroneously termed civilization. It does not apply to the wild tribes that have not been tinged and tained with the flase blessings of so-called civilization.

In our work titled "Kingdom of Heaven" we mentioned the "Uncanny Powers of Indians" of South America, and showed that some of them enjoy the resurrection and activation of the rare sixth and seventh sense powers exhibited by the Ancient Masters.

Of course the number in this class is small, and they are they only who live most closely in harmony with cosmic law, and conserve for their own use and development the extra flow of Solar Quintessence into the body's creative centers.

This produces brains instead of progeny, and results in the exaltation of such men to the angelic plane of intelligence and consciousness

The Masters discovered that the basis of this possible exaltation lies in the conversion of sexual force into a higher order than that of animalistic propagation.

This is the secret meaning, sometimes hidden and sometimes obvious, of many occult teachings, of theories of alchemy, of various forms of mysticism. This is the Philosopher's Stone.

The Masters discovered that the utilization of this creative force for body development and not for propagation, builds in man's Solar Body the power that exalts him to the high level of Seership.

There is no other way. There is no other force in the universe than can replace the Creative Force of the body for that purpose. Or for the purpose of getting the sidh well for that matter.

THE CREATIVE FUNCTION

What department of the body possesses the power of creative work? The procreative centers.

Can the creative work of that department be diverted and directed to any other purpose than that of producing progeny? That question we have considered above under the subtitle of Seership.

The power of Seership is the result of the creative function being diverted from the producing of progeny, and directed to that most high purpose of increasing brain activity and nerve force, thus producing the super-state of

Cosmic Consciousness.

Long ages ago the Masters discovered that the habit of masturbation weakens the mind and produces imbeciles.

This discovery led to the logical conclusion that if the dissipation and consumption of the Solar Quintessence weakens the mind, the conservation of it would strengthen the mind.

They found that when the body's creative work is changed from the production of offspring to the building of brain and nerve power, a marked change appears in every department of the body, and most especially in the improvement of the brain and nerve system.

Out of that discovery, thousands of years ago, rose the great school of the Ancient Mysteries, and that school produced the great men of the ages.

As great men are most difficult to enslave, the tyrants of all ages hated and opposed these schools; and their final destruction was at last accomplished by the work began in the fourth century by Constantine the Great, when he founded for that purpose the Roman Catholic Church.

The express purpose of the establishment of that church was the destruction of the Ancient Mysteries. The job was done, but to do it cost the lives of more than seventy million people.

CHAPTER VI

SEX FORCE

What does science know about Sex Force?

In physiology, the function of the sex, cells, the mystery of the sex-elements in the process of creation, was little understood half a century ago, and not fully understood now.

Until comparatively recent times it was considered improper to devote any study to the sexual phase of humanity.

Pruriency went so far as to set the phenomena of sex beyond the scope of legitimate investigation, and those who gave it thought and study were looked on askance and with suspicion, and their work was often submitted to ignorant and prejudiced moral censors, who, by their unfair action, added to the obloquy under which this subject rested.

The hidden theme of the Bible is Sex Force, the most colossal force in the universe, with dual aspects, -- (1) creative and (2) destructive.

In the Bible the creative phase is symbolized by the White Serpent, and the destructive phase by the Black Serpent, as explained in our work titled "The Magic Wand."

The destructive phase is symbolized by the Black Serpent of Temptation in Genesis, and by the Great Red Dragon in the Apocalypse, that "stodd before the woman which as ready to be delivered, for to devour her child as soon as it was born" (Rev. 12:4).

The destructive phase is also symbolized by the False Prophet, that tempts mankind by producing temporary pleasure while destroying body and mind.

The Four Beasts, so often mentioned in the Bible, always refer to the Sphinx, and the Sphinx always symbolizes the Four Principles of creation, viz., fire, air, water and earth, as shown in our work "The Mysterious Sphinx".

The Four Principles include the creative action of the Sun and that of the human body. For man is a creator no less than the Sun is.

Now, the way for man to be redeemed, or to redeem himself, from the low animal level of sexual generation, is to be raised up to the angelic level of rigid continence, as taught by the Masters, as explained in our work "The Great Red Dragon", and as so amazingly shown by Dr. G. R. Clements in his outstanding works, (1) "Science of Regeneration," and (2) "Virgin Birth".

That is the true and esoteric interpretation of the "resurrection of the dead" (dormant) so often mentioned in the Bible, and the esoteric meaning of the statement:

For in the resurrection (when man is raised up to the angelic plane) they neither marry, nor are given in marriage, but are (free of animal passion and lust) as are the angels (Mat. 22:30).

The gospel Jesus is made to say "It is not good to marry" (Mat. 19:10). Pol said, "It is good for a man not to touch a woman" (1 Cor. u:1). And again Jesus is made to say:

All men cannot receive this saying, save they to whom it is given. For there are some eunuchs, which were so born (remained virgins); and there are some eunuchs, which were made eunuchs of men (by castration); and there be eunuchs which have made themselves men   eunuchs (castrated themselves). He that is able to receive it, let him receive it (Mat. 19:11, 12).

HINDU VERSION OF SEX FORCE

Hindus portrayed the collosal power of Sex Force in a curious fable woven around their great god Siva.

With Brahma and Vishnu, Siva was master of the universe, his own function being generation and aiding new life to emerge out of death (dormancy), like Spring out of Winter.

It was Brahma himself who said, "Where is he who opposes Siva, and yet is happy?"

But Siva was not happy; for he was bereaved of his mate, and was tired and weary. So he wandered thru the land and came to the forest of Daruvanam, where the sages and their wives lived.

When the sages saw the great god Siva so haggard and sad, they treated him with scorn and saluted him only with bent heads.

Sica, tired and weary, asked only for "alms". Thus the god went about begging along the roads of Darauvanam.

As the women looked at him, they felt a pang in their heart. Their minds were perturbed and their hearts agitated by the sensations of love. They forsook the beds of the sages and followed Siva.

As the sages saw their wives following Siva, they pronounced a curse upon him:

"May his lingam fall to the ground."

The curse was effective; his lingam fell to the ground, sticking upright in the earth, but Siva himself was gone.

As the lingam fell, it penetrated the lower worlds. It grew and grew until its top towered above the heavens. The earth quaked. The lingam became fire, and caused conflagration. Neither god nor man could find peace or security.

So both Brahma and Vishnu came down to investigate and to save the universe.

Braham ascended to the heavens to ascertain the upper limits of Siva"s lingam, and Vishnu betook himself to the lower regions to discover the depth.

Both returned with the report that the lingam was infinite: It went lower than the deep and higher than the heavens.

And the two great gods both paid homage to the lingam, and advised man to do likewise. They further counceled men to propitiate Parvati, the goddess, that she might receive the lingam into her yoni.

This was done, and the world was saved.

Mankind was thus taught that the lingam is not to be cursed nor ignored; that it is infinite in its influence for good or evil; and that rather than wishing to destroy it, they should worship it as part of the creative principle, and learn how to overcome and control its force of temptation (Sacred Fire, p. 92).

If we were not kept in darkness, if we were not deceived from childhood on, if we knew what the Bible actually teaches, we would then not regard it as the dead "word" of a mythical god, but as a scientific treatise of the Ancient Masters on the Creative Force of the human body, portraying and presenting over and over, in symbol and parable, in many and various ways, from the Serent in the Edenic Garden to the Great Red Dragon of the Apocalypse, both the Good and the Evil, the Constructive and the Destructive, phases of the Great Force of Man, so infinite that it goes "lower than the deep and higher than the heavens."

CHAPTER VII

FOURTH DIMENSION

Can two or more objects occupy the same space at the same time without interfering with each other?

We are conscious of the space occupied by our bodies, and not conscious of other things, substances, elements, or forces occuping that same space at the same time.

To the average man, Time is a passing thing, and Space is a place occupied by a three dimensional object. To a scientifically trained man, Time and Space are only relative.

Imagine yourself at a telescope capable of seeing a man on a planet one thousand light years distant. You see a man on that planet seated at a telescope looking at you. You see him wave his hand, apparently at you.

When did he wave his hand? How long ago did the event occur that he was looking at? Now you have what? You have three periods of Time in the same space at the same time.

What you saw took place one thousand years before you saw it. What he saw took place two thousand years before the Time you sat at the telescope.

You have present Time, Time one thousand years ago, and Time two thousand years ago, all in one time and all in the same place.

We are not ordinarily conscious of the radiant forces in and around our body; but delicate instruments register these forces.

We do not know that the human body is an ideal receiving antenna for radio impulses, broadcast by a distant radio station.

Disconnect your radio aerial and have three or more persons join hands, then let one of them put his finger on the antenna post of your radio set, and it will prove itself.

By analogy at least, this radio force and your body are occupying the same space at the same time, yet you are entirely unconscious of the presence of these radio impulses.

Times as here used is as the average man perceives it, as is also Space. In connection with this, the student should read our work titled "Kingdom of

Heaven" in which we have devoted considerable space to Telepathy, Television, and the Fourth Dimension.

Knowing the existence of the forces occupying the same space with the body, we shall consider that radiant force, visible to some, surrounding the body, called the Aura.

We are now informed of the successful photographing of the human aura on the thin film of silver oxide.

The use of certain color screens shows that there may be many small auras in different bands of the spectrum that make up the body aura under proper screening. Why should the sodium band photograph to the exclusion of the other parts of the spectrum?

By analogy, we must conclude that whatever color is visible in the aura, that chemical in a vital state must also be present in the body.

We have produced radiant force, capable of being measured at least to a degree.

A more thorough and complete knowledge of the brain system, endocrinology, body aura, and Kundalini Force, will give the key to many strange things about the human body.

Numerous experiments have proven that we can control the functions of the ductless glands and choose whatever combination we want to put into operation.

Let us apply some of these experiences, together with cold logic and laboratory tests to some of the endocrine operating Triads.

The Love Cycle--Pituitary, Thymus, and Gonads, a pure physical love. When youth begins to bloom and feels the urge to procreate, he is in love. The following experiences have been experienced by most of us:

1. Pituitary Gland: All mental pictures of the opposite sex are beautiful and kindly.

2. Thymus Gland: All sensations in the heart region are loving and gentle.

3. Gonad Glands: The sexual organs are stimulated and an urge to copulate is present.

The Pituitary regulates physical functions, growth, bony structure, metabolism, chemical compounding, etc., and even the thoughts, emotions and the senses, under the control of the Black Kundalini.

The Thymus regulates the sensations, heart beat, breathing, etc., under the control of the Black Kundalini.

The Gonads regulate glycogen, lactic acid, semen, sex desire, etc., under the direction of the Pituitary, which is controlled by the Black Kundalini.

In a word, the operation of all endocrine triads or cycles on the physical plane are under the control of the Black Kundalini; while all the fourth dimensional, or what we term functions on the solarical plane, are under the control of the White Kundalini,--and all are under the control of the Mind.

If we disturb the function of any one of the glands forming the triad, that disturbs the other two. Let one of the parties wilfully interrupt the process of copulation, and what occurs?

The mental pictures immediately change. The loving sensations of the (heart) Thymus turns to anger, disgust, and we see defects in our partner that before we did not notice.

The copulatory organ of the male relaxes and becomes useless temporarily for procreative purposes.

The Fear Cycle,--When we experience fright, the Pituitary, Thymus, and Suprarenal glands form a working triad and become active.

The Pituitary, under direction of the B.K., directs the sense organs to ascertain the cause of the fright; the Thymus causes increased heart action, blood circulation and breathing, and the Suprarenal glands excrete additional adrenalin into the blood, preparing the muscles to flee or fight.

When the Pituitary has ascertained that there is nothing to fear, the Suprarenals cease to supply more adrenalin to the blood, and in their place in the triad, the Pancreas is substituted, but working with the Parathyroid and Spleen, forming a five grand cycle, or triple triad, under the control of the Anahata Chakra.

The white corpuscles of the blood begin to collect the excess adrenalin for elimination from the body. That is the reason why many patients and persons desire to urinate after fright, sometimes emptying and collapsing the bladder after a severe fright shock.

SOLAR MAN

The human body is physical, but he who dwells therein is inherently Solarical. Or we may more correctly say that he is a Fourth Dimension Being, occupying the same space with the body at the same time.

Scientific instruments disclose the fact that the inner, solarical, or fourth dimensional man exists on a vibratory plane far above that of the body.

Most scientists are agreed that all visible substance is solidified solar force, and that all force is an invisible substance. The only difference being the vibratory rate.

Experiments show that when the Love Cycle is changed over from Pituitary (negative, female), to Pineal control (positive, male), that changes the spectrum colors of these glands.

We recognize chemicals by their respective color bands in the spectrum.

When the Gonad glands radiate dark red under Pituitary and Black Kundalini control, and are changed over to Pineal and White Kundalini control, the dark red color disappears from the Gonads, and a pink color, bordering on orange, shows in place of the dark red.

This is a striking illustration of the Power of Mind over Matter. Here is the evidence to prove it.

When the Mind is switched from Carnality to Solarity, from earth to sky, when we transfer Mind from the Love Cycle to the Life Cycle, when we change our thoughts from animality to angelicality, from the animalistic plane of Lust to the angelic level of Life, we observe how we are helped and how completely that changes the control of the Creative Function of the body from the Pituitary and Black Kundalini of animality, to the Pineal and White Kundalini of angelicality.

The ultimate result is, that instead of man's consuming his precious Solar Essence in the purely animal function of procreation and or pleasure, he conserved the vital essence for the exalted purpose of body and brain improvement.

THE SECRET WORD

The Mystic Number Four,--Card 4 of the Egyptian Tarot, representing the Emperor, the Great Law of Four, the Secret Word, the Inerfable Name,--discussed at length in our work titled "The Mysterious Sphinx" (p. 19).

This was the secret four-lettered name which the masses were forbidden to pronounce; the "Lost Word" of Freemasonry, once known to but few, and finally lost, and a temporary substitute for it adopted (p. 453).

We noticed in "The Mysterious Sphinx" its elementary symbolism, and now go deeper into the Lost Wisdom of the Ancient Masters and consider the most esoteric phase of the Sphinx symbology.

The Mystic Number Four related to the Four Principles of Creation, and its deeper aspect related to the Four Principle Glands of the body chiefly involved in the Creative Process. These are:

1. Pineal, Fire (Solar) center of the brain
2. Pituitary, Air (Psychic) center of the brain
3. Prostate, Water of Life (Semen) center of the body (Rev. 21:1)
4. Gonads, Bull, Earth (animalistic production) center of the body.

These are the Four Fixed Signs of the Zodiac, the Four Elements of Creation and also of Redemption, and the top secret symbolism of the Sphinx which referred to the Redemptive Process.

In "The Great Red Dragon" we mentioned the Tarot, and included Card 6, Temptation, referring to the Edenic Garden, environed by soft blue hills, in which were Man and Woman, with a tree of golden fruit, and a serpent that whispered in the woman's ear.

In that parable the Serpent symbolized the Black Kundalini Force which controls the Pituitary gland in the function of animalistic propagation.

Tarot Card 6 was also called "The Lovers" and pictured a young man, with two women, standing at a point where two reads meet, symbolizing the Two Paths of physical existence, one being the strait and narrow way which leads to Health and Happiness, and to this path one of the women was pointing, while the other woman pointed to the broad road that leads to the City of Destruction.

The Path of Health and Happiness is uphill all the way, with the Crown of Health and the Throne of Longevity at the top.

The Path of Destruction is downhill all the way, with ill health (hell) and early death (grave) at the bottom.

Man is a free agent, and has the power to choose his path,--and it is given unto him according to his choice, for he reaps as he sows (Gal. 6:7).

MIND POWER

Ye are transformed by the renewing of your Mind (Rom.12:2)

We have just observed how the Power of Mind can drag man down until he is lower than the beasts, or exalt him to the Blue of the Sky.

The power of Mind over Matter enables man to overcome the strong urge to propagate on the animalistic plane by switching the Mind from the earth (bull, hell) to the sky (Sun, heaven).

Then a change occurs, in a moment, in the twinkling of an eye. The Temptation to copulate is gone; and a New World instantly unfolds before us,--a Garden in a green valley, surrounded by soft blue hills, filled with trees bearing golden fruit, which represents the redemption of Solar Man to the high plane, where they neither marry, nor are given in marriage (Mat. 22:30).

This act of the Mind, the most colossal force in the universe, is the great step on the uphill path that leads to the Higher Life; and that is what Paul meant when he said, "Ye are transformed by the renewing of your Mind (Rom.12:2).

This is the real transmutation of the body's Creative Force from the animalistic to the angelic plane, and results in the exaltation of man far above the low level of animalism. For that purpose is the reason why he possesses greater intelligence than the lower animals.

When man thus voluntarily and consciously begins to live on a higher level, that will cause the resurrection of his dormant organs, and the result is that awakening of the unusual powers called Cosmic Consciousness (p. 244).

GOLDEN AGE

Do not turn to science for help in this work, for science has nothing of value to offer. The great Carrel wrote: "Men of science know not where they are going. They are guided by chance" (Man the Unknown. p. 23).

Those who base their opinions upon the faulty premises of conventional science, fall into one of the greatest errors by indirectly assuming that the category of cause and effect, in which natural phenomena are placed, is complete in itself, and therefore completes the cycle of human reason.

That is grossly erroneous. The fact of the matter is, that it requires (1) end, (2) cause and (3) effect to complete the cycle, and not just cause and effect alone.

The End may be termed the (1) origin of cause and the (2) goal of effect, beginning and ending in the same source, thus completing the cycle.

Unless the End or Purpose is included and considered, there is no rationality in the thought.

Where can the End of creative work be found outside of Man? Of all created things, in Man alone is the purpose and the end of creation presented. For Man is the highest creation, and that means the end thereof, as we explained in our work titled "Pre-Existence of Man".

Granting that this is so, then the controlling factors of the biological and physiological characteristics of Man must necessarily lie within Man himself as a primary and ultimate proposition, and in Nature only as a secondary factor, or only insofar as Man has degenerated below the standard of original perfection thru the abuse of reason, instinct, and his own body.

The reader should here be informed that on practically every page of any standard work of Physiology, we find more or less theory, assumption, and speculation as to the purpose and function of various structures and organs of the body, many of which little or nothing is yet known, and some more or less dormant and rudimentary.

Darwin was one of the first scientific investigators in modern times to show that the human body contains many dormant and rudimentary glands, the purpose and functions of which are utterly unknown.

After studying the human body for forty years, the great Carrel said: "In

-56-

fact, our ignorance (of the body's functions) is profound" (Man the Unknown, page 4).

Darwin sought to account for the presence of these dormant and rudimentary structures by assuming, without evidence, that they are the vestigial and rudimentary remains of the stuctures that were once useful in an earlier progenitor, but useless now because man has progressed to a higher plane.

In other words, Darwin assumed that these dormant and rudimentary structures are "hang-over appendages from the ape days of man". A very preposterous course for any scientist to pursue in his effort to explain what he does not understand

It never even dimly occurred to Darwin that the reverse is the true situation. That in reality, man has regressed instead of having PROGRESSED.

Fragments of ancient records show that the Golden Age man was vastly superior to the stone age man, the iron age man, and the modern machine age man..

In order that the world would have no knowledge of the Golden Age Man, when the Roman Church (Catholic) was founded by Constantine the Great in the 4th century, it began a systematic, vigorous campaign to destroy all ancient records and literature for the express purpose of plunging the world into darkness, and making man believe that he had been on earth but a few centuries, and had sat in darkness until the gospel Jesus, the alleged Light of the World (Jn. 1:7-9), appeared in 325 A.D., only 1631 years ago, as shown in our work titled "Mystery Man of Christianity".

Be it known that the said Jesus was not born of any Virgin in the first century, but was a character invented by the church fathers in the 4th century,--a gigantic fraud which the church has attempted to conceal by the destruction of libraries, the burning of literature, and the murder of men.

NEW VARIETIES

In his attempt to account for the presence of these strange vestigial and rudimentary structures in the body, Darwin resorted to the processes of variation and modification, formulating the Law of Modification in these terms:

1. Organic bodies exposed to changed conditions undergo definite modification.

2. When modification of structure or constitution appears in the parent, it is transmitted to the offspring in an augmented degree.

3. By the process of modification it is possible to produce new varieties.

And these "new varieties" being nothing more nor less than the degenerate descendants of more perfect progenitors, are regarded by science as a superior type of man. But that makes just as much sense as does the theory of evolution.

When we base our conclusions on facts, we should know that we have all the facts and not just some of them. We should also know that facts have no significance when disconnected and separated from the conditions, circumstances, and the ultimate purpose for which they can be of service in our work and which determine their value.

A fact in itself alone has no value. It is just a bald fact. Facts must be properly and consistently corralated to be of any value.

Should some scientist find any of these statements difficult to reconcile, how else can the true significance of some of the biological and anatomical findings of Darwin and Wallace, Spencer and Fiske, Huxley and Haeckal, with reference to the rudimentary and dormant structures in the body of man, be explained, determined, correlated and accounted for?

We explained in our work "Pre-Existence of Man" that something cannot come from nothing, and the greater cannot come from the lesser. Progress is the great fact of all ages, but progress beyond the Original Source is an impossibility,--the dream of a disordered mind, and there are many of them.

As something cannot come from nothing, then of necessity that source from which things come, must be the equal at least of all that comes. Also, that which comes describes with great clearness the character of that from which it comes.

Then, in order to form a better picture of the Superior Being from which modern man has descended, we must restore to their original, natural condition and function, the vestigial, rudimentary and dormant structures of the body,--- glands and organs the purpose of function of which modern science knows nothing.

CHAMPTER VIII

THE FOUR PRINCIPAL GLANDS

The Pineal, Pituitary, Prostate and Gonads are the four principal glands involved in the creative processes of the body; and while they have been noticed, they are so important that they need more attention.

The Pineal comes first and last. This gland is a puzzle to science. Being utterly ignorant of its purpose and function, it is quickly dismissed as being just an atrophied eye that was perhaps useful to an early progenitor, but entirely useless to modern man because "he has progressed".

While science knows nothing of the purpose and functions of the Pineal, it has recently discovered about the Pituitary some of the things which the Ancient Masters knew five, ten, perhaps fifty thousand years ago.

The Pituitary is the Master Gland of the Endocrine System in body construction, and therefore it was symbolized in the Bible as Zerubbabel, "The Builder of the Temple" (body) (Zech. 4:9).

The Pituitary, thru the psychic body, controls the involuntary functions of the physical body. To that end it excretes potent hormones which control and prod the other glands into action.

The Pituitary regulates the physical functions, growth, bony structure, metabolism, chemical compounding, etc. Even the thoughts, emotions, and senses of man on the physical plane are under its control. So, when the Ancient Masters termed it "the builder of the Temple", they knew its functions.

The Pineal is attached to the back and lower part of the third cerebral ventricle, which extends forward and downward and into the stem (infundibulum) and rear part of the Pituitary. The ventricle forms the gap that exists between the two glands.

At the Pituitary end of the gap is the Throne of the Psychic Body, and at the Pineal and is the Throne of the Solar Body.

The Pituitary does not, in the regular activity of the body and its glands, execrete, as a rule, the particular hormones that effect the Pineal on the Solar Plane until the activity of the Pituitary has been stimulated and intensified by the rising Solar Fire from the creative centers at the base of the spine. And if the Solar Fire is consumed in copulation and masturbation, it is gone and not there to rise up and stimulate the Pituitary.

When the Pituitary is thus stimulated, then its vibratory rate is increased, the current of force from it grows stronger, and when the current has deflected sufficiently to contact and activate the Pineal on the Solar Plane, the gap between the two glands is bridged, the circuit established, and the goal of Retemption has been attained.

The Pineal is the organ of memory, expectation and anticipation. It never forgets, and even contains all the wisdom of past ages.

It was theactivation of the Pineal by hypnotism that enabled Bridey Murphy to go back one hundred years and review and relate events of her antecedent incarnations. She was hypnotized by Morey Bernstein and was able to recall having lived in Ireland one hundred years before. The startling story appeared in many papers and periodicals in 1955, and was published in book form in 1956.

A. R. Martin, of Sharon, Pennsylvania, claimed no psychic gift, but he was able to take the seeker back into antecedent experiences. The person saw and felt such remarkable things that he forced to believe that they were events which occurred in his former lives, or that he subconscious possessed increible powers.

Martin majored in psychology at college, made a study of hypnotism, and became interested in the work of Dr. Cannon, who could send the subject's memory back to the moment of birth, but no farther.

Martin published a book, "Researches into Reincarnation and Beyond", in which he recounted some fifty of his thousands of cases.

Not every subject could be sent back through time. The ability to relax physically and mentally is vital.

An orthodox preacher visited Martin, and was taken back through some of his previous incarnations. Some of the experiences caused him to burst into tears, and he asked whether it were conceivable that he had lived thru so much.

Martin replied, "If all that were not there in your mind, it could not be coming out."

The preacher saw himself in the past as a ruler of a 10th century Chinese province. During this review, he lectured on Buddhism, changing in Chinese. Later he saw himself in a Swiss chalet as an old men, futiely trying to comfort a distraught daughter.

In all instances, his present physical body assumed, as if by magic, the posture, tone and bearing suitable to the character he believed himself to be.

Once he appeared to suffer such agony from thirst that a doctor, in the room could hardly be restrained from administering to the "dying" man.

But when he woke up he did not want a drink.--Condensed from Fate Magazine.

Some psychologists hold that these visions are caused by contact with Universal Mind rather than by personal experience. We must remember that the Superconscious Department of Mind is a phase of Universal Mind.

This is the Kingdom of the Solar Man of the Masters, that sees and knows all things, and forgets nothing.

PITUITARY TUMORS

Walter Timme, M.D., of New York City, in 1934, presented to the American Neurological Association some findings showing the connection between Psychic Trauma and Pituitary Tumors.

Dr. Timme recited some strange information concerning the vital relationship of the pituitary and the act of copulation that should be known to every person. He said:

"It is a quite prevalent idea...that if during intercourse the occurrence of the orgasm can be prevented, conception will not occur. As a result of this, it is not surprising to find that innumberable instances come to the attention of the physician of such attempts at inhibition.

"In this particular group of patients now to be described, numbering five, a frank confession of the desire to be free of the results of intercourse was made, and the method to attain such freedom was to prevent the orgasm from occurring at the critical juncture.

"In each case there was added the interesting and important statement that this attempt at inhibition was made with all the 'mental power' that could be brought to bear in order to delay the orgasm.

"And further, that suddenly during this attempt, there occurred a queer feeling in the head, as of something tearing or breaking within it, accompanied by sever pains, and, in two cases, of nausea as well.

"In all of the five cases, within a few days following, there was noticed a gradual change of feature, beginning in four of the cases in the face, with a gradual spreading and enlargement of the malar (cheek) bones. In the other cases, the change was one of beginning obesity,

"These changes were rapidly progressive, in four to a distinct acromegaly (a disorder that enlarges the bones of the extremities), in the remaining one to a market pituitary type of obesity.

"Two of the cases went to sugical intervention, with the removal of a pit-uitary adenma (glandular tumor) in the one, and the finding of an inoperable pituitary mass in the other.

"One died, refusing operation, of what was indubitably a pituitary neoplasm (abnormal growth, as a tumor), with all the classical signs and symptoms,

"One disappeared from observation, but not before x-ray examination of his skull and a complete physical status was compiled, giving certain evidence of a pituitary neoplasm.

"and finally, one is still alive, acromegalic in the extreme, with no advance of the condition, but with frequent headaches and visual disturbances.

"Of the five cases, four were women and one a man. Three of the cases were unmarried. The ages at with the initial symptoms were inaugurated were all in the 20s and or early 30s.

"To summarize therefore: Five cases are presented, four women, one man, who developed pituitary neoplasma following directly upon what might be called psychic trauma, called forth by psychic inhibitory attempts to avoid the organism of intercourse. "

Timme mentioned experiments on the pituitary, viz., those in which a slight induction current sent through the base of the brain at the pituitary caused ejaculation in rats; that directly after intercourse, or soon thereafter, the urine contains large amounts of anterior pituitary-like substance, all of which goes to show the enormous effect of the interaction between the pit uitary and copulation.

THE PROSTATE GLAND

The Prostate, third gland in the tetrad, is located near the base of the back-bone. It is larger than a hen's egg, and contacts the lower part of the bladder, and thru it passes the urethra as it leaves the bladder. Science knows little about this gland, its purpose, its functions, or the purpose of its excretions.

The ejaculatory tubes of the gonad glands enter this gland. and between it and the pubis is the rich venous pudendal plexus, in which ends the dorsal vein of the penis.

The Yogins call this gland the Kanda, and term it the seat of the Kundalini Power. To function on the solar plane in relation to the Pituitary and the Pineal, the gland must be in a normal, healthy state.

What are the facts? Here we find that man has not progress as science thinks.

In most elderly men the gland often hypertrophies, and not infrequently calcarous concretions are found embedded in it, --all resulting from bad habits.

In many men the gland is affected by a disorder termed prostatitis, which is a frequent complication of gonorrhea. In very few men is the gland found any where near a normal, healthy state.

An oily fluid is excreted by the Prostate, which is subject to varied degrees of consistency, from a thin, volatile oil that promptly evaporated when exposed to the air, to a fixed oil that produces permanent stains on paper.

It is this oil that stains the linen in cases of nocturnal emissions , which occur in men who have weakened their creative centers by early masturbation and sexual excesses.

In healthy, wise, vigorous men, of which only a few are found, the fluid is a fixed oil. In the average man it is more or less volatile. In young men of dissolute habits it becomes filthy. In "rakes" is very malodorous and may con-tain pus..

Here is the seat of the terrible veneral disorders that afflict mankind. Listen to what we are saying here, all of you who think about Cosmic Consc-iousness. You rise to Cosmic Consciousness thru your glands, and we are trying to explain how it is done. If your glands are incompetent to function on that plane, then Cosmic Consciousness is a state beyond your reach.

To attempt to teach people with defective glands the secret of the Solar Fire is a waste of time and effort. And this is the kind of people of which most of the multitude is composed.

This oil, excreted by the Prostate, enters the blood and is carried all over the body. It is one of the basic constituents of the blood, and, in its purest state, the Greeks termed it Chrism.

Then came the cunning church fathers. When they compiled the New Testament to advertise their actor Christ, to play the part of the Solar Fire, they labelled everything good as "Christ" to deceive the masses.

And so the Greek "Chrism" became the Blood of that Christ (Heb. 10:19; 1 Pet. 1:2; Jn. 1:7). It also came to be called "the Christ in man" (Col. 1:24,27).

More fraud and falsehood. Those who rejected these bibical frauds in the dark ages were condemned by the church and burnt.

The Prostate consists of muscular and glandular tissues, and has twelve to twenty ducts which pour their product into the blood,—and into the urethra under the stimulation of masturbation and copulation. Then it is dissipated, waster, and the cost thereof to the body is very great indeed.

This milky fluid, discharged under the influence of erotic thoughts, nocturnal emissions, masturbation and copulation, is largely supplied by the Prostate, with some help from the Cowper's glands.

These excretions constitute the liquid portion of the Life Fluid called semen; and while it is necessary to sustain the life of the Spermatozoa, it contains none. They are elaborated by the gonads.

WHEEL OF LIFE

It is well to pause and notice that the zodiac (zodiakos) is derived from zodion, "a little animal" and a diminutive form of zoon, "an animal", of which zoa is the plural, a word that goes directly back to Slermato-Zoa, the Fluid of Life and its Germ of Life.

The semen is excreted by the Prostate as stated, and the Zoa by the Gonads. Thus we observe that the Zodiac of the Masters was rightly called the Wheel of Life, because its twelve signs were represented by little animals that symbolized the Zoa of the Semen, the Life Essence of the Body, with the Zoa elaborated and excreted by the Gonad Glands.

Here is the evidence to prove that the ancient zodiac was correctly called the Wheel of Life; that it was closely and directly connected with the Life Fluid and the Life Glands of the body, and that it had nothing to do with an anthropomorphic God in the sky.

SOLAR FORCE

In Yoga literature the Kanda is said to be a center of the astral body. From it rise thousands of tiny nadis, termed astral tubes and composed of astral substance, extending out to the various organs and glands, carrying solar force, vital force, nerve force, Prana, all synonymous terms (Kundalini Yoga, p. 40).

In modern man the currents are exceedingly weak, due to dissipation, the degenerate condition of the body, and of these special glands in particular.

Solar Force, as Solar Liquescence, flows thru these nadis, which are composed of astral substance, and are beyond the reach of material science; so no test-tube experiments in any laboratory can be made of them on the physical plane. For that reason science rejects as pure superstition all the Ancient Masters said on the subject.

No test-tube experiments in a laboratory can be made of the Mind either, but who will deny the existence of Mind? It is known by its work, and so are the nadis (p. 216).

GONAD GLANDS

The Gonads are the foundation of the mystic tetrad. In man they are contained in the scrotum, exposed to all sorts of damaging conditions, and presenting further evidence of degeneration.

In his Science of Regeneration, Clements shows that the male scrotum is formed by a union of the lips of the female vulva and their expansion into folds, leaving a raised seam (raphe) that divided the scrotum into two parts.

Clements contends that the testes appear as herniated overies, with the positive element of the ovaries developed to a functional degree, while the negative element is rudimentary and astrophied (p. 47).

In supporting the doctrine of human degeneration, Dr. Bernard Rackow wrote:

"If Dr. ------ were wise enough to approach the subject of the Virgin Birth Debate thru the proper channel of reasoning, he would observe whay may appear to be a flagrant inconsistency of Cosmic Creation in placing the most important glands (testes) of the body in the scrotum, and supported by a few weak cords, in an exposed position where they receive the least protection of any organ or gland. This fact becomes a matter of grave significance in explaining the remost past of Man as to his bisexual origin" (Virgin Birth Debate, 1936).

The gonad glands rule the ductless gland system. They rule the brain of most men. As a men thinketh so is he (Prov. 23:7). Degrading are his thoughts whose brain is governed by his gonads.

Whose ever looketh on a woman to lust after her bath committed adultery with her already in his heart (Mat. 5:28).

This is the reverse of what should be. Yet that is the common condition of man. He should rule his desires, but most men are ruled by their desires, not for good but for evil.

The brain, the Mester of the body, has become the slave of the gonads on the carnal plane   And the God of all the earth, created to have dominion over all living things (Gen. 1:26), has become a lowly degenerate, ruled by lust and led by those who preach spirituality and yet live on the lowest plane of materiality.

The gonad glands were also called "the destructive glands" by the Ancient Masters. They function for life or death, depending on the set of the lever. Their propagative function perpetuates the race; but in that process man sacrifices in no small degree his own self. Much worse is his dissipation of his Solar Essence for pleasure only.

The gonads are under the control of the lowest chakra, the Muladhara (root support), at the root of the spinal column (Meru), and also the Svadhishthana, the prostatic gland, where the positive and negative currents of the Solar Fire start when it is not dissipated and consumed in masturbation and copulation. It corresponds to Sagittarius of the Zodiac, hence its rider is the Bowman.

In this sign the Romans placed Deana, the Greek Letois, Apollo's sister, who was sometimes pictured as a bearded Goddess. Together they represented the male-female or androgynous man, the original bisexual creative unit.

The Svadhishthana chakra belongs to the lowest of the somatic divisions; yet as the White Horse, that division outranks the others, because it is the starting point of the Solar Fire, in the absence of which the other chakras would remain semi-dormant.

The Bowman, Apollo-Diana, is the Conqueror himself (Solar Man), who is here represented as going forth conquering, and to conquer (Rev. 6:2).

This esoterically means, that as the rising Solar Fire activates each chakra, it is said to conquer that chakra, and to increase in power as it rises, growing ever stronger as it ascends, and striking the Ajna chakra at the Pituitary with such force, that the shock, as it passes on to the Pineal, sets it into action, producing those effects on the physical and psychic man that are described in symbol and parable in verses 12 to 17 or chapter 6 of Revelation, and in chapters 7 to 11.

The student should review several times the statements here made as to the general condition of the four principal glands involved in the creative processes. Then he will realize why the masses can never rise to that high, solaristic state of Cosmic Consciousness.

These higher sense powers, rarely encountered in modern times, depend upon the proper function of normal endocrine glands, consisting chiefly of the gonads, prostate, pituitary and peneal. The function of the latter is unknown to science, but was known by the Masters to be "THE ORGAN OF SPIRITUAL SIGHT" (Voice of Isis, p. 316).

The pineal is dormant or semi-dormant in civilized man, and the pituitary is ruined by the effects of masturbation and copulation.

No matter how good the condition of the pineal may be, it cannot perform its high function of activity on the fourth dimensional plane without the aid of a normal pituitary, the female, negative pole of the solar fire.

The facts are that the endocrine glands, the functions of which augment man's state of consciousness, are in a state of lethargy and degeneration in the average man in civilization.

To stimulate and activate the endocrine centers to a higher state of function, and thus improve body and mind and increase the life-span, was the object of the secret teaching of the Masters.

CHAPTER IX

RADIATION

What the Ancient Masters knew about Cosmic Radiation is being partly discovered by modern science.

Some twenty-five years ago the last Sr. James Jeans, F. R. S., was one of the first scientists to call attention to the impact of cosmic rays upon man. He wrote:

"Cosmic radiation falls on the earth in large quantities. .Every second it breaks up about twenty atoms in every cubic inch of our atmosphere and millions of atoms in our body, and we do not yet know what its physiological effects may be".

The late Prof. R. A. Millikan, one of America's foremost physicists, in 1935, said:

Cosmic radiation is "raining enormously energetic bullets of some kind (photons, electrons, or both) from all directions upon the heads of mortals who live on the earth."

In 1940, a prominent British physician wrote: "We know almost nothing of the effects of man of cosmic radiation."

The human body receives radiation and emits radiation. Science has measured the radiant force emitted by the roots of onions, carrots, etc. It has found that radiant force emitted by the human eye can kill yeast cells, yet no other part of the body seems to emit such killing rays.

As we apply our knowledge and scientific instruments to the study of radiant forces emitted by man's body, the discoveries are amazing.

The brain is divided into three sections: cerebrum, cerebellum, and medulla oblongata, with two obes each, making six lobes comprising the brain.

Science has discovered that the left lobe of the cerebrum controls all our willful movements of the right side of the body, while the right lobe controls the left.

The left lobe of the cerebellum controls all our unconscious or automatic movements of the left side of the body, the reverse of the function of the cerebrum. But medical text books teach nothing concerning the functions of the medulla oblongata in its relation to brain function.

POLARITY

The negative pole of the cerebrum is situated along the outer rim of each lobe, and the positive pole is situated along the center line of each lobe, where they join.

The negative pole of the cerebellum is situated along the center line of each lobe, and the positive along the outer rim, the reverse of the cerebrum, thus accounting for the left lobe of the cerebrum controlling the willful movements of the right side of the body, while the left lobe of the cerebellum controls the unconscious movements of the left side of the body.

The negative pole of the medulla is located at the lower end of the spine, between the last vertebra, fifth lumbar, and the coccyx, and the positive pole is situated just above the atlas of the spine, where the head swivels on the spinal column, the thyroid gland region, the cavernous nerve plexus, ruled by the Vishaddha Chakra, the highest of those belonging strictly to the sympathetic system.

INTELLIGENCE

Knowing that the radiant force incessently emitted by the body, called the aura, and at different frequencies, some capable of killing yeast cells, and, properly screened, showing throughout the entire spectrum from infra-red to ultra-violet, that the rate of vibration or cycles per second of some of these rays are so rapid as to be beyond any known instrument,--we are ready to consider the finding of science that:--

Of the some fourteen billion brain cells within man's head, the most intelligent of us use less than ten percent of our capacity, the inevitable being that we are all of us at least ninety percent ignorant. That our conscious powers are only ten percent of what they should be. That it is possible for our consciousness to be increased ninety percent. That is the road to Seership.

The low conscious powers of the average man is astounding. The psychological department of the U.S. Army conducted an intelligence test of the soldiers in World War I, and was surprised to find that the average soldier showed a mental capacity of a 13-year-old child.

The tests showed that, of the men of the various branches of the service, the engineers stood at the top, the veterinarians at the bottom, and the medical next to the bottom.

The engineers are taught to use their brain and think, but the medical doctors are taught not to use their brain, as all of their thinking has been done for them by the medical hierarchy. And beyond that line of thinking they are cautioned to go only at their own risk, the penalty for so doing being the revocation of their license to practice their art.

The Ancient Masters, not bound by any standard of professionalism or commercialism, and whom modern science terms superstitious heathens, had reached that stage where the better training of the intellect enabled them to bring into action many millions of those unused brain cells, so long dormant in the average man, by means of the activation of a strange power that is traceable all thru ancient religious teachings as the Kundalini, "The Mother of the Universe."

This was the top secret of the Ancient Masters which the church fathers were determined to conceal at all cost; so they destroyed the ancient scriptures, which dealt with the subject, after using them to make their Bible to support the power of the church and to enslave the masses.

The wanton and deliberate destruction of libraries, manuscripts, scrolls and other ancient records is a fact presented in modern history; but the reason for this destruction has always been well concealed.

It is a little known fact that the Vatican has the most complete library of ancient literature than any other institution on earth. The church fathers took the ancient records they considered too valuable to destroy, and hid them from the masses.

In our work titled "Cosmic Creation" we have shown that all cosmic processes are creative processes, making death a creative process no less than birth.

Cosmic radiation is a creative process. As we breathe we inhale the creative essence of the universe. Some call it vital electricity; the yogins call it prana.

The creative essence fills the entire body, is carried by the nerves, and called nerve force. The brain is the station of control and direction.

The raw creative essence is refined by the glands and prepared for creative work in the body, and is used for all purposes, two of which are (1) to create a new person, or (2) to sustain and rejuvenate the body, increase brain power and augment the consciousness.

We must sacrifice much to propagate on the animal plane. We gain much if we take the other path.

THE MAGIC WAND

What is the insignia of medical art? A staff entwined by two serpents, at the top of which is a globe with wings.

This is the very ancient symbol of the Kundalini, the Solar Fire of the body, a description of which is well-covered in our work titled "The Magic Wand".

The Kundalini Force is a part of man's communication system, as well as a powerful directing force of the brain function.

That force can be traced by instruments from the base of the spine to the brain, and shows two seperate frequencies.

Can Knowledge of the use of this force be disseminated to the world at large? Yes and no. Only to a very small class, and it if for them that we write.

This work is intended only for those who can concentrate-analyze, think and reason.

Electricity is one of man's most useful agencies. The generators, motors, solonoids, condensers, robots, light, heat, radio, radar, television,--and yet electricity is a dangerous force if improperly handled, and will kill as quickly as it will serve mankind.

Experiments over periods of many centuries have shown that the Kundalini Force is as deadly as electricity, and vastly more benefical and useful to mankind when properly handled.

Why do ancient writings refer to the Kundalini as the White and the Black Kundalini? The answer is found in the answer to why brain matter is white and grey,--grey being only a shade of black.

According to science, the sole food of the brain is oxygen and lactic acid, which is assimilated by the white brain matter, and that the grey (black) brain matter regulates the glycogen and prevents ketones from entering the brain system.

Experience has shown that we should put little faith in what science says about such matters; for overwhelming evidence proves that science knows nothing about the forces and processes of the body. The great Carrel wrote: "In fact, our ignorance (of the body's forces and functions) is profound" (Man the Unknown, p. 4).

The latest findings on nutrition, based on recent evidence, is to the effect that the body is composed of cells, the cells are composed of atoms, the atoms are composed of electrons, and electrons are whirling centers of electricity in the ether. These facts rule out the theory of nutrition.

Advanced physiologists assert that food does nothing more than to stimulate and activate the body cells, passing thru the body and leaving it without ever becoming a part of it.

What would save man from becoming a hog if he ate hog flesh and it became a part of his body? This subject is well covered by Kenyon Klamonti in his work titled "The Nutritional Myth."

Let us assume that oxygen and lactic acid are the only known elements which stimulate and activate the brain cells. Oxygen comes from the air, and lactic acid is derived from chyle, a milky fluid formed from chyme by the action of the intestinal fluids.

CHAPTER X

LIGHT OF THE WORLD

Dr. V. G. Rele, in his book "The Mysterious Kundalini" says that the Ida and Pingale Nadis, previously mentioned, are the left and right sympathetic nerves, and the Sushumne is the spinal cord.

Other authorities hold that the Sushumna is not the spinal cord, but is a nadi inside the cere bro-spinal structure next to the spinal marrow, is composed of etheric substance, and is in the center of the Royal Road, the Brahmanadi, the "tube" thru which the true Kundalini Force ascends from the sacral plexus, the Mulhadara Chakra.

The Susnumna is the central staff of the Caduceus, represented in the Bible as the gospel Jesus crucified between two thieves, the letter representing the Ida and Pingala nadis (Lu. 23: 32).

The Sushumna is uniform, erect, starts at the Mulhadara as the Filum Terminale, passes thru the other chakras as it ascends, and as the Tantric text expresses it, "sparkles like a string of jewels." For the Yogins say that the Nadis are "luminious arteries" of changing colors, depending in color on the Pranic (solar) force flowing thru them.

The Sushumna is said to enter the Ajna chakra between the eyebrows, and extends upward to the Pineal gland in the brain, and on to "Brahmarandhra," which means "the hole of Brahma," or soft place in the crown of a baby's head, later obliterated by the growth of the head bones.

Starting at the Svadhishthana chakra, the prostatic plexus, the Ida and Pringala ascend to the Ajna chakra in the forehead, but with an inverse serpentine movement which causes them to wind from right to left, and inversely, surrounding the Sushumna and the chakras, but not passing thru the chakras as does the Sushumna.

The properly constructed Caduceus shows these two intertwined nadas as two serpents, a black one (Ida, evil), and a white one (Pingala, good), and the areas where the two serpents should cross the wand (Sushumna) are the points where the chakras are located in the body.

In the spinal nerve system three different forces have been discovered, each on a different frequency, two of which can be registered and traced by instruments, but the third, as it nears the Pineal, is soon beyond the range of all scientific instruments. Its vibrations have been estimated to be in the billions of cycles per second.

Some assert that this third force is the real Kundalini, the current entering the Sushumna at the Muladhara chakra (root of the spine), and that the Sushumna does not energize until the force of the Ida and Pingala has reached the forehead. So the two thieves were crucified with Jesus to make the picture complete.

This third force, we are told, is actually the product of the blending and intensification of the other two, which increase in power at each chakra on the ascension, then return to the sacral plexua and enter the Sushumna at the Muladhara, flowing upward and activating the chakras as it flows.

The Sushumna rises and crosses the base of the skull and contacts the Ajna chakra at the Pituitary back of and between the eyebrows, then passes upward to the Pineal, below the thousand-petalled Sahasrara of the "Brahmarandhara," the crown of the head, called the "above of Shiva," by the Yogins.

The Pineal gland is electrical (positive, male), and is connected with the Pingale nadi, which crosses the spinal cord at the base of the skull in the medulla oblongata, and extends down the right side of the spine to the Kanda (Prostate, Svadhishthana chakra).

The Pituitary gland is magnetic (receptive, female), and is concected with the Ida nadi, which crosses the spinal cord at the same point as the Pingala, and extends down the left side of the spine to the Kanda. Then thru the semilunar nerve ganglion the Ida and Pingala merge into the solar plexus.

The pneumagastric nerve, rising in the fourth ventricle of the brain and connected with the cerebellum, crosses the spinal cord at the base of the skull where the Ida and Pingala cross. It sends branches to the throat, lungs, heart, thymus, stomach, etc., and ends in the solar plexus, the abdominal brain, consisting of twelve large nerve ganglia, sometimes symbolized in the Bible as the Twelve Tribes of Israel.

The solar quintessence of creative quality is refined in the kanda and the gonads, and when not consumed in masturbation or copulation, it flows up the Sushumna and returns to its Throne in the brain. So Jesus, as a symbol of the Life Essence, "was received up into heaven, and sat on the right hand of God" (Mk. 16:19),

As the Life Essence ascends the Sushumna (the ascension of Christ), it makes the crucial crossing at the base of the brain (crucifixion of Jesus before being received up into heaven), and returns to the optic thalamus, where it undergoes a final refining process, and is then transmuted into the Golden Oil (Zech. 4:12) which is deposited in the "crystal lamp", which represents the optic thalamus.

This is the oil referred to in verses 1-12 of the 25th chapter of Matthew.

The bridegroom mentioned there represents the Pineal gland in the brain (heaven).

BIBLICAL SYMBOLISM

These secrets of the body and its functions are allegorically mentioned in Zechariah.

The two olive trees represent the Ida and Pingale nadis (vs. 3).

The hands of Zerubbabel (Pituitary gland) have laid the foundation of this house (body); and his hands shall also finish it; and thou shalt know that the Lord of hosts (Solar Man) hath sent me to you (Physical Man) (vs. 9).

Zerubbabel with those seven (seven chakras); they (chakras) are the eyes of the Lord (Solar Man), which run to and fro through the whole earth (Physical Man) (vs. 10).

What are those two olive trees (Ida and Pingala) upon the right side of the candlestick (Sushumna) and upon the left side thereof (vs. 11).

What be these two olive branches (Ida and Pingala) which thru the two golden pipes (Ida and Pingala) empty the golden oil (Solar Quintessence) our of themselves (vs. 12).

These are the two anointed ones (the two witnesses), that stand by the Lord (Solar Man) of the whole earth (vs. 14).

This precious fluid, the golden oil, the Solar Quintessence, supplies the nerves that dip into this bowl (optic thalamus) from the cerebrum, and when this occurs, it produces that sudden shock of Light at the Ajna chakra (Pituitary) which passses on to the Pineal, and resurrects millions of dormant brain cells, resulting in that peculiar phenomen of glorification, illumination.

When this occurred, the neophyte became an Epopt, a Seer, and the shock caused him to cry out, "Hail, New-Born Light, I am initiated and become holy!" (p. 522).

If the body is in good health, if the solar chambers have not been ruined by polluted air, if the ductless gland system is in normal condition, then when we raise up the solar fire, the precious oil, by saving it, the substance becomes so hightly refined, transmuted and vitalized, that it activates all the seven seals, including the pituitary and pineal glands in the brain, and produces that high state termed Cosmic Consciousness.

As the rising solar fire (jgolden oil) reaches the brain, it first activates the pituitary, the feminine, negative pole, causing it to send a stream of bluish solar electricity thru the infundibulum to the pineal, the male, positive pole, thus completing the circuit.

The Bible calls this "the marriage of the Lamb", and purposely presents the

-72-

fable so as to make it appear to mean the marriage of the church to the gospel Jesus (Jer. 7:34; 16:9; 25:10; 33:11; Rev. 18:23; 19:7; 21:2).

As this stream of vital electricity activates the dormant pineal, then the brain becomes filled with Solar Light.

So, Jesus, as a symbol of the Solar Light, is presented as the Light which lighteth every man that cometh into the world (of regeneration) (Jn. 1:9).

The process is regular and natural. It could be no other way. The availably literature on the subject, coming largely from India, is very confusing, showing that the yogins have either purposely misled the unwary, or have themselves been groping in the dark.

NATURAL FUNCTION

To illustrate how regular and natural are these higher functions of the body, we should remember that migratory fowls need no man-made compass to direct them to their destination. The radio and television mechanism in their head serves that purpose.

These fowls can see Cuba from Canada, just as Apollonius saw Rome from Ephesus, and fly there in the fall to spend the winter.

Nor do these fowls need to be taught these things. They are regular, natural functions of their organs which are provided for that purpose.

Man has the same equipment in his head, but it is crippled and ruined by bad air and bad habits. The electric chambers and the radio and television mechanism begin to sink in degeneration when he has his first cold as a little child. Then followed the sinus ailments as ahe grew older.

We cannot teach man how to use what he has that is useless to him. And if it were in a useful state, it would perform its natural functions without any special training

All we can do here is to inform the reader what he should have, and explain the reasons why he does not have it.

No one can be taught how to use one's crippled, ruined, and useless equipment. Nor do we claim to be able to do that.

CHAPTER XI

MOTHER OF THE UNIVERSE

In his work, under above title, Rishi Singh Gherwal first gives the location of the Kundalini Power, then says that man has several bodies, but confines his statements to the Sthula (gross) and the Sukshma (subtle) bodies.

-73-

The gross body can be felt but the subtle body cannot. It is the body we are in when dreaming, when we are temporatily in the fourth dimension plane and "there should be Time no longer" says the Bible (Rev. 10:6).

These two bodies are kept together by ten pranas; five are subtle and five are gross. The gross pranas are in the gross body and flow thru the gross Nadis or nerve system. The subtle are in the subtle body, and flow thru the subtle Nadis.

The student should be informed that these pranas are nothing more nor less than various phases of solar radiation.

These two phases are connected with the heart, which is the organ of sensation. When poets and others felt that sensation, they called it Atma (God) in the heart.

These details are erroneous. The heart is not an organ of sensation. It is the great central valve of the blood ascular system, controlling the flow of the blood. The organ of sensation in the heart area is the Thymus gland, of the endocrine system, as we have explained under that heading.

The other connection of the pranas is between the heart and the navel, and that is the mind.

More error. The great nerve gnanglion in that region is the Solar Plexus, called the abdominal brain, and controls the involuntary functions of the body under the direction of the Subjective Mind centered in the brain.

The subtle body has as many nerves as the gross body. The three major ones are the Ida, Pingala and Sushumna, the latter located between the Ida and Pingala.

"Electrons are the building blocks of the universe " said Millikan.

Electricity is electrons in transit. Air is composed of free electrons, which are of two kinds,--positive and negative.

The right nostril absorbs positive electrons, and the left, negative. When we close the left nostril and inhale thru the right, we inhale positive electrons and they flow down the right sympathetic nerve trunk.

When we breathe alternately and rhythmically thru right and left nostrils, we charge the electric battery in our body, whose poles are the right and left sympathetic nerve trunks that lie on each side of the spine. When their electric polarity is strong enough, a spark or current flows between them at the Muladhara chakra, consisting of free electrons, which hit the nuclei of the atoms there, and release intraatomic force, called Kundalini Power, Serpentine Fire, etc.

The Ancient Masters discovered that when this force is not consumed in masturbation or copulation, then it folows up the nerve trunks of the spine, causing an intensification of the action of the chakras, the cells of the battery.

Finally, this power rises up to the Pineal gland in the brain, which is then resurrected by the force to clairvoyant activity. The entire brain becomes radioactive, and this is mentioned in the Bible as the Single Eye that fills the whole body with Light (Mat. 6:22).

Those who rose up from the ranks and became the leaders of humanity on the higher plane of consciousness, were those in whom this internal power was consciously wielded. Their brains radiated that mysterious force by the means of which they were able to see things not seen by the masses.

The difference between a superman and an idiot is the difference in the brain. The brain of the former is better developed and charged with more solar electrictiy, and radiates more powerful waves.

The chakras are etheric vortices of power that are connected with the six major sympathetic nerve plexuses of the body and the seventh in the brain. They are semi-dormant in those who live on the animalistic level of propogation because the force by which they should be activated, is consumed in masturbation and copulation.

The Ancient Masters taught that when the spinal column and nerve system are normal, and the body becomes regenerated, and there is complete conservation of the Creative Essence, all the sympathetic nerve plexuses (chakras) become vivified by the ascending Serpentine Fire, and when this force reaches the brain, it resurrects into conscious activity the Pituitary and Pineal glands, the organs of psychic hearing and seeing, clairaudience and clairvoyance.

In the living brain, the Pineal is phosphorescent and glows with a radiant light. This is the inner eye of the body, hence the meaning of the saying, "If thine eye be single, thy whole body ;will be full of light."

The Pineal has the structure of an eye, with photo-sensitive cells that respond to the finer ultra-violet rays. It is an organ of the fourth dimensional vision, where there is no Time-Space element, and when resurrected, enables one to behold a new fourth dimensional world, the astral world inhabited by the super-human denizens of other planets.

We sometimes dream in a few minutes the events that fill a whole lifetime of Time. A drowning person reviews a lifetime of experience in a few seconds, because, for that short space of time, he has passed out of this thirddimension and is temporarily in the fourth dimension plane where there is no Time as we know it.

When the creative essence of the sexual centers is conserved, it is converted into brain substance and electric energy, as it is chemically of the same nature as the brain substance, both being rich in lecithin, cholesterol and organic phosphorus.

Since the most ancient times it was known by the Masters that the life glands elaborate a vital substance which, if retained within the body, rises up to the brain and improves the brain and nerve cells.

Four thousand years ago Hindu doctors were grinding up dried generative glands into powder and giving it to their patients in the hope of restoring youth and vigor.

Dr. Serge Voronoff became world famous for his experiments in transplanting the sex glands of monkeys to human beings for rejuvenation purposes.

These men knew that dynamic vitality owes most of its power to the Life Essence producted by the Creative Glands at the base of the spine, and yet men continue to waste and squander it in masturbation and copulation (Kingdom of Heaven, p. 31).

When Kundalini flows up the spine, it activates and vivifies in turn each chakra, thereby causing these etheric vortices to rotate at terrific speed, and etheric energy to flow into the corresponding nerve centers and endocrine glands.

Some assert that when Kundalini becomes active, the body becomes etherialized and a new Solar Body is born in place of the old gross body of heredity, and this is the Redemotion or Rebirth.

Others hold that this is erroneous. They contend that the Solar Body is present from the first, and is the real man. But the manifestation of the Solar Body is below par because the physical body is below par. To intensify the manifestations of the Solar Body requires the improvement of the physical body.

It is this low condition of the physical body that dormantizes the chakras and weakens the brain nerve system. It is the physical body that needs building up, and not the Solar Body.

VIRGIN BIRTH

The Bible says that men were giants in the Golden Age, and were called "The Sons of God" because, no doubt, they were virgin born (Gen. 6:2, 4; 1 Jn. 4:9).

And in the Grand Cycle of Life the Golden Age will dawn again, when man obeys the commandment not to eat of the "forbidden fruit," and the Great Red Dragon in the blood has been conquered, and that colossal force reversed from creating children and flooding the land with mental weaklings, to that of creating Brains and filling the land with Mental Giants.

The Ancient Masters correctly taught that man sacrifices himself in producing children; and that when he conserves his Creative Essence he is exalted far above the animal level of sexual generation.

At this point the authorized version of Revelation says, "And there shall be no more curse" (22:3).

In the original Greek it read: "And the accursed (function) shall not exist any more."

This indicates that in the case of Eternal Solar Body, the Real Man, the "accursed" function of sexual generation does not exist. For that function is strictly nothing but an animal function, and can never be anything else.

CHAPTER XII

SOLARICALISM

In this work we are presenting the new doctrine of Solaricalism.

In our previous works we have observed the common terms of spirit, spiritual, spirituality, and spiritualism.

In this work we have discarded these meaningless terms, and used the terms solar, solarical, solaricality, and solaricalism,--all of which refer to the Sun, the cosmic source and Father of all.

People like to be fooled, and reject things they can understand. They love the spiritual terms because they cannot understand them; and will turn away from the solarical terms because they can understand them.

That we know, and that constrained us in the past to employ the spiritual terms. But in this work we have adopted a new policy and turned from the empty words that actually mean nothing, and replaced them with words that have a real meaning back of them.

All of our days we have heard talk of the Life Principle, and no one who used the term knew about what he was talking. Science has searched for the Life Principle, and knew not for what it was searching.

If man is an electric machine, as the works of Burke, Baines, Crile, Flechner, Gradewitz, Grunewald, Littlefield, Ousterhout, Veraguth, Viala and many more able scientists have clearly shown, then man is not a Spiritual Being but a Solarical Entity.

He is a Son of the Sun as the Ancient Masters declared,--a fact recognized by the biblical makers when they wrote that man is a Living Soul,--the term Soul coming from the word Sol.

That doctrine makes snes, and most all phases of it can be clearly proven by overwhelming evidence.

The Solar Orb has been recognized and reverenced as the Creator by ancient races back to the remotest periods of man's existence, as shown in our work titled "Ancient Sun God".

Aristotle said, "Man and the Sun generate man, making the Sun the common Father of all manking."

Men is all ages have expressed in words, thoughts, and emotions their dependence on the Great Globe of Light on which we. no less than they, depend for everything, including our Life (p. 28).

History shows that all ancient races traced their origin back to the Sun and the Father of the Jewish race was Ab-Ram, the Sun God of the Chaldees.

During the seventy years of Babylonian captivity, the Jewish priests had lots of time to dtudy Babylonian tradition, and thus they discovered the legend among these ancient people to the effect that all great races and all great men were descendants of the Sun God.

So, in harmony with this ancient legend, the priest Ezra, who wrote the first five books of the Bible, invented the story of Ab-Ram (Most High Father-- Sun), and Sa-Rai (Moon Goddess), and began his fable with the 12th Chapter of Genesis in order to have it agree also with the Twelve Constellations of the Babylonian Zodiac, and thus have his Ab-Ram connected with that ancient Wheel of Life.

"For a father of many nations have I made thee" (Gen. 17:5), were the words that Ezra attributed to the Sun God and directed to Ab-Ram. And the words were literally true, for the Sun is indeed the Generative Principle of the Universe; and so - Abram, the Sun God, was actually the "Father of many nations and Races" (Ancient Sun God. p. 26-7).

MORE PRAISE FOR PROFESSOR HOTEMA

"I am most pleased with the new spiral binding on the last few books I purchased from you. The ease in handling while reading in my opinion help keep these books in perfect condition longer than the old way of glue and stitching which in time loosens up and causes pages to separate." Marie Glenda, Los Angeles, California.

"I have just read Prof. Hotema's "The Land of Light", which you recently sent me. It is a wonderful work. Of course it made me want all I can get of Prof. Hotema's folios." -- M.C.P., Petaluma, Calif.

"My wife and I have completed your Hotema Folio, for the second time. If I could be granted one wish for the greater good for the human race it would be ....that every man and woman should read this folio at least once.

"We have been members of the Rosicrucian Order for many years, and the lessons and instructions covered many of the things in the folio, and prepared our minds for a better understanding.

"You refer to work which is more completely covered in your complete course of study, prepared from data gathered from the Temple of the Masters. How can we become eligible to make this complete course of study of the Ancient Masters? -- George O. Keefer,, Los Alamos, New Mexico.

"I have just finished reading "Man's Higher Consciousness," by Prof. Hilton Hotema. I think it is a most wonderful book. I think it is the whole truth. I wish I had the information it contains earlier in my life. Many thanks to Professor Hilton Hotema. -- Edmond Groben, Indiana.

"I am an old subscriber. I have purchased most of the Prof. Hotema folders and even all of the Kenyon Klamonti series sometime ago. They are all really very well thought out and presented so simply that even a child could understand. Hurray for simplicity."

"Please send me a list of other Hotema writings published by you. At last we have a writer who knows what he is talking about." -- F. S. K., Glens Falls, N.Y.

"Your book, 'Cosmic Creation' is very great. Veil following veil is lifted and more and more must be known of Creation.
" 'Whence came all the INTELLIGENCE in the first place to create and to organize? What Master Mind is there back of it all to know?'
"Thank you very much, and I will order your books as I receive notice of their publication. I don't want to miss anything.' == G. R., Modesto, California.

"Truly, Hotema is a great man. My husband and I were privileged and blessed with five vistis with him, and he has done more for us, just to sit and talk with him, than anyone else has ever done.
"It would seem that Hotema has been sent by the Great Creator to reveal strange facts of the world to blind and darkened people. He is a great teacher, a giant of wisdom.
"From his breath and body there emanated a fragrance like that of a fragrant flower, showing that it was not corrupted by eating the products of the dirty barn yard, pig pen, and slaughter house.
"Please send the books as soon as possible." -- H. P., Cathedral City, California.

WE APPRECIATE BEING APPRECIATED - Testimonial Letters From Our Customers

"Gentlemen;
     "During the past few months I have read in amazement 10 books by Professor
Hotema (all that your distributor - the Omangod Press had available).
     "I had studied and read many books on health, nutrition, religions, oriental
philosophies, metaphysics, occult and all related subjects for the past 35 years. I
was under the impression that I was pretty well informed on these subjects so I wasn't
prepared for the impact I received from Hotema's books.
     "Not only did I feel a tremendous response in mind and soul but every cell of
my body seem to accept these profound truths. As a result my thinking has changed
considerably.
     "Professor Hotema mentioned several books in his works that I do not have. I
would appreciate your mailing me a complete list of all his books that are still
available. I will then purchase those I do not have.
     "Enclosed is a self-addressed stamped envelope for your convenience.
     "Thank you very much for your help in this matter." "Sincerely" Bertha C.
Berube, 3601 No. 6th Ave., Apt. 30-A, Phoenix, AZ 85013 (Sept. 10, 1981)
                    ****

"To Health Research,
     "I've bought your book - 'The Gospel of the Holy Twelve'; and after reading
it (with great pleasure), I beg of you, to inform me about - copyrights, clauses
and what else; because my intent is to make a danish translation (complete). I've
never tried such things before, and I presume - You know everything to be done.
     "My feeling is, that so many as possible should read this new Gospel, don't
you agree?" - Your's Sincerely, - Mr. Benny H. Nielsen, Mlktr., Svendelodden 15,
2, mf, 2400 Copenhager., NK Denmark. 21 sept. 1981
                    * * * * * * * * * * * * * * *

"Greetings,
     "Your organization was rated 'par excellence' in The New Consciousness Catalo-
gue by Nicholas Regush. He stated you were an excellent Mail-Order House with
Occult & Alternate Healing Methods.
     "I would like to receive one of your catalogs. Any assistance on this matter
would be appreciated. - Thank you." - T. R. E., Des Moines, Iowa 50312 (9/15/81)
                    * * * * * * * * * * * * * * *

"Gentlemen:
     "We think your Catalogue number 2A 1981 is Great. Please send us your whole-
sale book price list. Thank you." Sincerely, C. D., Aquarian, Sea Cliff, N.Y. 11579
(July 30, 1981)
                    * * * * * * * * * * * * * * *

"Dear Sir,
     "Recently I acquired the Nikola Tesla volumes that your organization researched
from the Interloan Library System here in Illinois. The research and detailed work
was very well done, thank you for this exquisite history.
     "Therefore, would you send me a catalog of all your works and all the investi-
gative reports you have done.
     "Please send price lists and mailing and cost directions to the below address.
     "Sincerely" - J. L. F., Champaign, Illinois 61820 (September 21, 1981)

The Masters who escaped death, were those who fled to island India, where their successors still abide in the fastnesses of the Himalayan Mountains, and whose ages are said to range from 500 to 1500 years. From that source there trickles the small stream of that Ancient Wisdom which Hotema presents in his various writings.

The author gives as his concepts and discusses in a general way the following: Daily exercise; vegetarian diet; raw foods; sun bathing; periodical fasting; deep breathing; history of longevity; cosmic forces; secrets of the ancient masters. Some of the headings taken from the book are as follow:

The Aging Process; Conditions of Artificial Life; Return Must Be Slow and Gradual; Antiquity of Man; How to Reverse Physical Appearance of Aging; Constipation the National Disorder; Does Man Starve; Finding The Truth; Food Stimulates; It Is The Body That Acts; People Who Crave Poison; Power of Adaptability; Fish Does Not Give Brains; Danger of --

Abrupt Changes; Men of Great Stature; Stature Originally Gigantic; Man's Body resembles Planetary Bodies; Misleading Reports; Body Craves Food, As It Does Poison; Man Eats To Die; We Eat To Live, and We Eat to Die; Chronic Auto-Intoxication; Body Tries to Maintain Balance; Vitality Increases; Eat Little and Live Long; Body Needs Minerals From Cosmic Rays; Sensation of Hunger; Eating is a Vicious Circle; Atomic Energy; Eating Poisons; Dangerous Narcotic From Juice of Poppy; Mice Unable to Live on Human Diet; Body Vitality Reduced; Cereals Are A Bad Food; Fruits Easier Produced With Less Labor; Earthy Salts Cause Old Age; Alimentation and Decrepitude; Carnivorism is Bad; Fresh Fruit; Reason For Increased Vitality; Flesh Foods Putrefy; 48 Million Have Trichinosis; Mode of Living Builds Cravings, Aches and Pains; Opinions on Salt Eating; Table Salt; Longevity - hundreds of records; Fruit and Longevity; Doctors Do Not Live Long; Water Causes Aging; Live 200 to 300 Years; Less Minerals Needed After Maturity; Causes of Sclerosis; Lime deposits Cause Stiff Joints; King of Fruits; Spiritual Organs; Materialism Is A Superstition; Spiritual Intelligence; Man's Intelligence; Spiritual Powers; Ancient Science of Man; The Kingdom of God Within; Uncanny Powers of Indians; Man Is Dead As He Lives; Man Lives in The Spiritual World; Parthenogenesis (Virgin Birth); The Kingdom of God; Feeble Minds; Physical Purification; Function of Breathing; Shower of Red Mist (Blood); Breath Culture; The Skin; Exhalation; Breath of Death; Pernicious Anemia; Cerebral Hemorrhage; Causes of Cancer; Air is Life; The New Age; Eternal Physical Life; Breathe More -- Eat Less; Ionized Air; Why We Live and Why We Die; Man Eats to Die; Physical Perfection; Breath of Life; Stages of Degeneration; Magnetism; Spiritual Potentiality to Physical Actuality; The Way to Improve Physical Man; So Called Civilized View; Why The Truth is Suppressed; Economic Freedom; The Living Cell; Chiropractic Law of Physiology; Where Did the Living Cell Come From; Is Eating Necessary; Elimination; Cells Are Not Produced by Food; Early Men Were Breatharians; The Miraculous Cell; Physical Immortality; Why Man Degenerates; The Transportation System; Blood Purification; Vital Adjustment; Disease Germs; Good Health Is Not Immunity; Immunity Reduces Power to Resist; Conditions That Destroy Health; Danger of Smoking; Toleration by The Body; Immunity; Body Changes; Misleading the Multitude; Harmful Practices From Birth; Fewer Centenarians; The Body Fights Against Changes; Rudimentary Organs; Man's Natural Home; Altitude is Beneficial; She Eats Nothing; Survival Is Nature's Goal; Breatharrianism to Gluttarrianism; Buried Six Months and Lives; Spent Time in Cell; Materialism; Weight and Vitality Loss Due to Autointoxication; Live Without Eating; The Great Body Normalizer; Body Building Material; Discovery Amazed Material Science, etc., etc.

www.ingramcontent.com/pod-product-compliance
Lightning Source LLC
Chambersburg PA
CBHW071340290326
41933CB00040B/1879

* 9 7 8 1 6 3 9 2 3 4 4 2 4 *